# Margaret Fuller
## An American Romantic

# Berg Women's Series

| | |
|---|---|
| *Gertrude Bell* | Susan Goodman |
| *Mme de Staël* | Renee Winegarten |
| *Emily Dickinson* | Donna Dickenson |
| *Elizabeth Gaskell* | Tessa Brodetsky |
| *Mme du Châtelet* | Esther Ehrmann |
| *Emily Carr* | Ruth Gowers |
| *George Sand* | Donna Dickenson |
| *Simone de Beauvoir* | Renee Winegarten |
| *Sigrid Undset* | Mitzi Brunsdale |
| *Willa Cather* | Jamie Ambrose |
| *Elizabeth I* | Susan Bassnett |
| *Simone Weil* | J.P Little |

## In preparation

| | |
|---|---|
| *Dorothy Sayers* | Mitzi Brunsdale |
| *Rosa Luxemburg* | Richard Abraham |
| *Mary Wollstonecraft* | Jennifer Lorch |
| *Madame de Sévigné* | Jeanne A. and William T. Ojala |
| *Anna Freud* | Renee Paton |

# Margaret Fuller

**An American Romantic**

*David Watson*

**BERG**  *Oxford/New York/Hamburg*
Distributed exclusively in the US and Canada by
**St Martin's Press** New York

First published in 1988 by
**Berg Publishers Limited**
77 Morrell Avenue, Oxford, OX4 1NQ, UK
175 Fifth Avenue / Room 400, New York, NY 10010, USA
Nordalbingerweg 14, 2000 Hamburg 67, FRG

**British Library Cataloguing in Publication Data**

Watson, David
    Margaret Fuller. — (Berg women's series).
    1. English. American writers
    Ossoli Margaret Fuller, 1810–1850
    I. Title
    818'. 309

    ISBN 0–85496–181–X

**Library of Congress Cataloguing–in–Publication Data**

Watson, David, 1949
    Margaret Fuller / David Watson.
    p. cm. — (Berg women's series)
    Bibliography: p.
    Includes index.
    ISBN 0–85496–181–X : $35.00 (US.:est.)
    1. Fuller, Margaret, 1810–1850.   2. Authors, American — 19th century —
Biography.   3. Feminists — United States — Biography.
I. Title.   II.   Series.
PS2506.W37 1988
818'. 309 — dc 19
[B]
                                                                    88–4311
                                                                        CIP

Printed in Great Britain by Billings of Worcester

# Contents

# Illustrations

# Acknowledgements

Earlier version of my arguments about Margaret Fuller were presented in the spring of 1987 to the Humanities Department at Bristol Polytechnic, the third annual Colloquium on the History of Ideas at Middlesex Polytechnic and the Sociology Staff Seminar at Oxford Polytechnic. I am grateful to participants on all three occasions for their criticism and advice. The complete manuscript was read with immense care by my colleagues Frank Webster and Bob Woodings, and by Justin Dyer of Berg Publishers. All of their advice was good. I have taken most of it, but the responsibility for the remaining errors and inaccuracies must remain my own. I am also grateful to Miriam Kochan, commissioning editor for the Women's series, for suggesting that I contribute and then ensuring that I did.

*Margaret Fuller* was researched and written during a year of major upheaval and change at Oxford Polytechnic. The task was made enjoyable by the interest of colleagues and students and possible by the dedication and professionalism of the staff of two libraries. Oxford Polytechnic Library's inter-library loan team, lead by Paul Jeorrett, carried out all of my requests with speed and not a little imagination. When even they could not help I relied, as have a numberless band of researchers, on Mr. N. J. Hancock and his reader services department at the Cambridge University Library for their calm and courteous efficiency. Carol McCall and Cheryl Codling produced virtuoso performances on the word-processor. Betty, Sarah and Michael accepted Margaret Fuller into the family with curiosity and without complaint.

**David Watson**
Oxford
February 1988

For my mother

For my mother

# Preface

Margaret Fuller's importance can be measured objectively in several ways. She was a key figure in the history of American romanticism, in the transcendentalist circle, as a journalist and critic, and as a first-hand observer of and participant in the European Revolutions of 1848. The depth of several of these roles has only come to light as a result of modern scholarship and after a century during which if she was noticeable at all it was as a caricature. The mixture of suppression and appropriation leading to this situation obviously arose because she was female, and, in the broadest sense, a feminist. Margaret Fuller 'belonged', both in life and posthumously, to many other people, individuals as well as groups, each of whom with varying degrees of scrupulousness used her life and work for their own purposes. It would be a harsh but conditionally valid judgement to say that she herself helped to collude in these varied readings as a consequence of her own uncertainties about vocation and means of expression.

It has become a commonplace of both biographical and critical works to suggest that resolution of these dilemmas came, if at all, only in the last few months of her life, and that her death, along with her family and the loss of the notes for what she regarded as her most important work, robbed her of the opportunity to explain effectively what she had achieved and what she had become. Certainly the circumstances of her death, by shipwreck at the age of forty, gave dramatic impetus to the appropriation of her life and its meaning by friends and antagonists among her contemporaries as well by subsequent generations. Some outcomes have been bizarre, such as the modern scholarly attempt to establish, on the basis of psychohistory and the extremely patchy evidence about the foundering of the USS *Elizabeth*, whether or not her actions were suicidal.

If my book belongs to any genre it is to the rather old-fashioned one of the history of ideas. It can be argued that it is as much an attempt at recovery as any of those works which I criticize (and occasionally praise) below. I have, however, attempted to guard against the worst effects of appropriation by approaching Fuller's life and work from several angles. I have established as far as possible features of her hopes and achievements as expressed in her own terms. I have also tried to measure the effect of that life upon the intellectual and emotional lives of others. Finally, Fuller deserves to be taken seriously and independently as a contributor to historically important bodies of thought, and I have examined her roles as a romantic, feminist and a socialist. Disentangling the work from the life in this way is a complex but essential task.

In Part I I try to tell the story of Fuller's life, by reference to the domestic, social, political and intellectual circumstances in which she moved at various stages. I also attempt to explain some of the key choices which she made and which were made for her. Part II looks more systematically at the legacy of her published work, again in its immediate context, but also seeking an evaluation of its importance and influence over a wider span. Part III faces the hardest task presented by Fuller scholarship: an exploration of the manner and implications of her appropriation by her grieving comtemporaries and by subsequent generations. It will become clear that this has not been a history of progressive enlightenment, and that modern attempts at 'rescue' of the historically accurate Fuller do not always escape traps inherent in the entrenched historiographies which they oppose.

As the comments at the head of the Bibliography reveal, this is a work based almost entirely on printed and published sources. A little over a decade ago, before the publication of Bell Gale Chevigny's *The Woman and the Myth: Margaret Fuller's Life and Writings* (1975), this would have been impossible. Since then Fuller has become a minor industry, with the result that an almost complete and accurate corpus is now available to scholars. I am much in debt to the work of Chevigny, Robert Hudspeth, and of Joel Myerson in particular. The re-evaluation suggested above relies significantly upon their work.

# Part I  The Life

*Ralph Waldo Emerson*

# 1 Growing Up in New England

Margaret Fuller was born into a relatively distinguished Puritan family in Cambridgeport, Massachusetts, in May 1810. She was the first-born of Timothy Fuller (1778–1835), who took both the name and a reputation for political controversy from his father, and Margarett Crane (1789–1859), who gave up her short career as a school-teacher to marry in 1809.

The elder Timothy Fuller (1739–1805) had achieved notoriety for his dismissal by his congregation when he preached against the Revolution. When he was subsequently elected to a local convention to ratify the new constitution he then refused to support a document which allowed for the continuation of slavery. His five sons all became lawyers, including Timothy, who had been demoted in his Harvard graduating class for leading a student protest.

As a politician the younger Timothy Fuller served in the Massachusetts legislature and for four terms (1817–25) as a United States representative in Washington. Here he was strongly influenced by the democratic liberalism of Thomas Jefferson and attached himself to the party of Jefferson's successor, John Quincy Adams. Probably the highlight of his career occurred in 1826 when he hosted a party for the President in the large house in Cambridge, the Dana mansion (unkindly called 'Fuller's Folly' by his opponents), to which he had recently moved his family.

In national politics, however, Fuller and the Jeffersonians were on the losing side. Andrew Jackson's election to the presidency in 1828 represented a final defeat for the patrician, agrarian style of democratic politics symbolised by Jefferson's earlier victories over James Madison and the Federalists. Although modern political histories are careful to shade interpretation of a Jacksonian revolution in American politics (vote participation did not significantly increase, nor do state-level studies show Jackson's party to be the champion of the working class or the small farmer), Jackson's victory inaugurated a barnstorming, populistic style of politics which had no place for Timothy Fuller.

3

Fuller's early political ambitions, and then their disappointment, had a profound effect upon his family. In many ways the Fullers were typical of American upper middle-class families of their time. Margaret Fuller was the first of nine children, two of whom died in infancy. Her 'earliest recollection', recorded in the *Memoirs*, is of the death of her younger sister:

Thus my first experience of life was one of death. She who would have been the companion of my life was severed from me, and I was left alone. This has made a vast difference in my lot. Her character, if that fair face promised right, would have been soft, graceful and lively; it would have tempered mine to a gentler and more gradual course.[1]

Margaret's mother, whose name she chose to adopt (having been christened Sarah), sank into the background of family decision-making to an extent that, when Timothy died suddenly in 1833, Margaret, on whom his energies and hopes had all been fixed, took over the family at the age of twenty-five and did not begin to resolve her own vocational and emotional dilemmas until all of her siblings were established.

Their careers were conventional when contrasted with hers. The oldest brother, Eugene, became a lawyer and settled in New Orleans. The next, William Henry, who had turned his back on the farm at Groton, eventually succeeded as a businessman in Cincinatti. Her sister Ellen married the poet Ellery Channing, to the consternation of Margaret, who felt him to be talented but irresponsible. Perhaps the most famous of her brothers, Arthur Buckminster, who served as a conscientious editor of the posthumous works, died as a chaplain in the Union Army. Richard, to whom Margaret wrote frankly and movingly from Europe during the most difficult months of her life, became a lawyer. She nursed another brother, Edward, on his deathbed, while the final brother, Lloyd, was classed as a mental defective, for whom the family (principally Margaret) struggled to find a secure but benign regime.

Fuller's childhood and adolescence, for all its psychological conflict and trauma, was spent as part of the first generation of really settled middle-class life in America, away from the immediate rigours of the frontier (the closeness of which she was later powerfully to document in the travel book *Summer on the Lakes*).

She and her mother were thus beneficiaries and victims of what Barbara Welter and others have termed the 'Cult of True Womanhood'.[2] For working-class women and girls, early nineteenth-century industrialisation (more specifically the mills) provided a vocation of sorts and even a peculiar kind of economic independence. Those of the middle and upper classes were instead trapped into an idealised role as guardians of culture, civilisation and civility. As the contrast with the active male life of taming and exploitation of the frontier receded, the symbolism of the cult gathered pace and rapidly became enervating. Fuller's eventual escape from this less than gilded cage was one of her most potent achievements. Paula Blanchard, and others among Fuller's modern biographers, make the point that the psychological distress caused by Timothy Fuller's educational regime was not so much a problem in its immediate effects upon the adolescent, but more in the fact that it was not followed through. The vocation it might have promised was snatched away by his death.[3]

\* \* \*

Subsequently, Timothy Fuller has achieved greater fame for the way in which he set about his daughter's education than for any of his political achievements. Margaret was subjected to a full-blown classical education of the type which became the norm in late-nineteenth-century British public schools. She began to learn Latin at six, together with an initiation into the virtues of Roman republicanism which had inspired her father. Greek, which she began at ten, subsequently proved more congenial, but the hot-house effect of the regime took its toll.

Some powerful psychological pressures were at work here, including the unequal collision of an intense but disappointed father and a strong-willed and gifted child. Margaret and her learning became something of a showpiece in the Fuller's social set and it is not enough to remark, as did her friend Henry Hedge (1805–90 — later America's leading German scholar), that the curriculum was only unusual because she was a girl.[4]

Reviewing the evidence about Fuller's early education, and her subsequent reflections upon it, her modern biographers have tended to draw two sorts of conclusions, which can be mutually reinforcing. The first is about her relationship with her parents, reflected most crudely in Katherine Anthony's analysis of an Oedipal complex. The second concentrates on the perceived elements of 'masculine' and 'feminine' in her nature and how the former were reinforced by her experience in a social setting where they could never be satisfactorily acknowledged.[5]

Both themes are ever present in the most extended reflection which we have from Fuller herself, an autobiographical fragment from 1840 reprinted in the *Memoirs* (unfortunately the original does not survive, so the extent to which it may have been moulded by her editors is uncertain). In it Fuller characterises her parents: her father as a man of 'sagacious energy', but limited in his 'delicate and individual relations' to her mother and herself; and her mother, a 'fair and flower-like nature', who, of all persons she had known, 'had in her most of the angelic'. At this stage, however, the description of her experience at the hands of her father's ambition is almost entirely negative:

> Thus frequently, I was sent to bed several hours too late, with nerves unnaturally stimulated. The consequence was a premature development of the brain, that made me a 'youthful prodigy' by day, and by night a victim of spectral illusions, nightmare and somnambulism, which at the time prevented the harmonious development of my bodily powers and checked my growth, while later, they induced continual headache, weakness and nervous affections, of all kinds. As these again re-acted on the brain, giving undue force to every thought and every feeling, there was finally produced a state of being too active and too intense, which wasted my constitution, and will bring me, — even although I have learned to understand and regulate my now morbid temperament, — to a premature grave. . . . Poor child! Far remote in time, in thought, from that period, I look back on these glooms and terrors, wherein I was enveloped, and perceive that I had no natural childhood.

An escape of sorts was provided by her mother's garden, a constant motif in her accounts of childhood and early adulthood; in the family's many moves Mrs Fuller carefully dug up and transplanted her particular favourites.

> [Here] the best hours of my lonely childhood were spent. Within the house everything was socially utilitarian; my books told of a proud world, but in another temper were the teachings

of the little garden. . . . There my thoughts could lie callow in the nest, and only be fed and kept warm, not called to fly or sing before the time.[6]

The gloom of this and similar recollections is lifted somewhat by evidence of the social life of the 'youthful prodigy'. Putting aside such insecure comments as her twelve-year-old resolution to be 'bright and ugly', and the certain fact that not all who came into contact with her undoubted strength of purpose were charmed by it, the adolescent Margaret sought and achieved comfort, as she was to throughout her life, in some intense friendships. At this stage these included a strong attachment to an English visitor, Ellen Kilshaw, described in the 1840 fragment as her 'first friend'. In her teens she also benefitted from the interest and patronage of a number of older women, some of whom, like Eliza Farrar (1791–1870 — the wife of the professor of astronomy at Harvard, and the author of one of the age's most successful advice books, *The Young Lady's Friend*, 1836) sought explicitly to help her to adapt to society.

When Margaret reached her early teens Timothy Fuller sought assistance with her education. Between 1823 and 1825 she was sent to Dr Park's School in Boston, Miss Prescott's School in Groton (as a boarder) and Mr Perkin's Cambridge Port Private Grammar School (specifically because of its inclusion of Greek in the curriculum). Her request to her father that she be allowed to attend the Emersons' School for Young Ladies was ignored.

The effect of these excursions was not only to overlay Timothy Fuller's enthusiasm for the classics with modern languages and some extremely elementary science, but also to express further some of Margaret's social anxieties. In 1844 in *Summer on the Lakes* she published, somewhat incongruously, what has come to be known as the 'Mariana fable', a fictional account of an adolescent girl's estrangement from her fellow students at a boarding-school, her telling of lies and her planting of 'the seeds of dissension', leading to a confrontation and her breakdown. Most now agree that, if not a direct account of her experience at Prescott's, it at least arose from her experience there. What is most interesting is the idealised act of reparation and reconciliation (perhaps effected by Susan Prescott herself in reality) through which Mariana 'returned to life, but it was as one who had passed through

7

the valley of death':

> It was not long after this that Mariana was summoned home. She went thither a wonderfully instructed being, though in ways those that sent her forth to learn little dreamed of.
>
> Never was forgotten the vow of the returning prodigal. Mariana could not *resent*, could not *play false*. The terrible crisis, which she so easily passed through, probably prevented the world from hearing much of her. A wild fire was tamed in that hour of penitence, such as has oftentimes wrapped court and camp in a destructive glow.[7]

With the hindsight prompted by knowledge of her later life and work (which certainly influenced the editors of Fuller's *Memoirs*, who delight in pointing up premonitions and prophecies) it is hard to know exactly what to make of the accumulated evidence about Fuller's childhood and early education. Her own testimony, with its themes of resentment, guilt (which may have led to her recurring nightmare about her mother's death) and pride in her achievements, add force to interpretations, such as Chevigny's, which stress the function of many of her later acts as reparation, particularly for her mother.[8]

\* \* \*

In 1833 Timothy Fuller moved his family to rural Groton, his political career at an end. Here he failed conspicuously to fulfil a final ambition, to become a gentleman farmer like Thomas Jefferson.

Margaret deeply resented the move, which took her away from the intellectual circles of Cambridge and Boston in which she had begun to move with increasing ease and confidence. Several contemporaries regarded her almost as a honorary member of the Harvard class of 1829, as she formed friendships that were to influence her personally as well as intellectually: with William Henry Channing (1810–84), James Freeman Clarke (1810–88), Henry Hedge, and her glamorous cousin George Davis (1810–77).[9] Glimpses of the more stimulating life she was foregoing came in a trip with the Farrars and her friend the aspiring painter Samuel Ward to the vacation spot of Trenton Falls in New York (the funds for which she had to negotiate in detail with her father), as well as the first of her several meetings with the

British feminist and social commentator, Harriet Martineau (1810–76).

On her return she suffered one of the most severe of the spells of illness which blighted her life until her late thirties. It was after this that her father made a rare, and to her important confession.

My father, too, habitually so sparing in tokens of affection, was led by his anxiety to express what he felt towards me in stronger terms than he had ever used in the whole course of his life. He thought I might not recover, and one morning, coming into my room, after a few minutes conversation, he said: 'My dear, I have been thinking of you in the night and I cannot remember that you have any *faults*. You have defects, of course, as all mortals have, but I do not know that you have a single fault.' These words, — so strange from him, who had scarce ever in my presence praised me, and who, as I knew abstained from praise as hurtful to his children, — affected me to tears at the time, although I could not forsee how dear and consolatory this extravagant expression of regard would very soon become.[10]

Later that year Timothy Fuller was dead, a victim of the cholera epidemic of 1835, leaving his family tied into the kind of probationary tangle that affected large numbers of not particularly wealthy New England families at this time. Margaret Fuller's hopes of the career and independence for which her father might have been said to have prepared her were dashed, as were her plans for a trip to Europe. Given her mother's long-standing retirement into sweet ineffectuality, she was forced to take control of the family's affairs: to attempt to fight its battles with her stern and traditional Uncle Abraham as executor of the will; to tutor the younger children; and to prepare the older two of her brothers for Harvard. The contemporary separation of male and female roles and the 'cult of true womanhood' immediately exacted a personal penalty.

Beyond domestic management and home-tutoring, only one vocation appeared open and Fuller followed her mother into school-teaching. This, however, was school-teaching with a difference. Her first position, for which Ralph Waldo Emerson (1803–82) — who had been most impressed with Margaret on their meeting in 1836 — later took the credit, was as assistant to Bronson Alcott (1799–1888) at the latter's Temple School in Boston. Here she was to give 'instruction in the languages' and take over from Elizabeth Peabody the recording of what Alcott and Peabody had already published as *Conversations with Children on the Gospels* (1836).

Alcott, because of his longevity, seems at times a permanent fixture in the cultural history of nineteenth-century New England. Notorious for his 'Orphic Sayings' — epigrammatic 'intuitions' on a variety of subjects which provided good grist to the mills of the transcendentalists' critics — Fuller joined him at a point when his experimental school was approaching its period of maximum controversy. Essentially Alcott seemed to have abandoned all notions of formal instruction. He proposed that the truth of religion, including the interpretation of scripture, could be instantly intuited by the conscience, and that as a consequence the perceptions of the young and innocent would be the purest and most direct. Fuller's accounts of her experiences in the 'Temple' are full of wit as well as affection for the sage, but a combination of her delicate health, some pedagogical misgivings and the school's financial difficulties compelled her to leave in 1837, shortly before the school folded (in part as a consequence of Alcott's insistence on taking in a black child).

Her next position, with the Greene Street School of Hiram Parker in Providence, was more remunerative and extended. However, the same pressures of health and family obligations intruded and she left her last formal teaching post in December 1838. Here, some of her female pupils have left evidence of how they came to idolise her. Feelings were reciprocated. In a manuscript note, collected by Chevigny, she indicates her particular concern for the girls in her charge and how poorly they had been prepared to fulfil the intellectual capacities which were properly theirs, and not just a male preserve:

> I gave some idea of the barbarous ignorance in which I found them, appealed to their remembrance, and told some facts in confirmation of these extraordinary statements. I showed them how all my efforts had, necessarily, been directed to stimulate their minds and prepare them for discipline, and how I had been obliged to leave undone much that I should, under other circumstances have deemed indispensable.[11]

Exhausted though she was by personal and professional commitments, Fuller maintained her personal and intellectual links with her Harvard friends, several of whom were now beginning to scatter, and began to be looked upon by key figures as a resource, especially in terms of her growing knowledge of German, and of Goethe in particular. Her first publication, in which her father took great pride in the last year of his life, had been an anonymous defence of Brutus, against attacks on his character and motives by the prominent historian George Bancroft (1800–91). In Goethe, and German Romanticism in general, she found a broader cause to champion.

During the years at Groton, encouraged by Hedge and Clarke, she had ambitions to write a biography of Goethe, and worked as intensively as she could on him, preparing translations of his *Torquato Tasso* and his conversations with Johann Eckermann. Through the mediation of her friends she was even permitted to use the Houghton Library at Harvard, the first female scholar so honoured. In Goethe and the other early German Romantics (especially Novalis, Schiller, and Richter) she found kindred spirits for her own empathetic misgivings about the apparently pale and over-intellectualised revolt of the early transcendentalists. While sympathetic to the movement in its search for a satisfying moral and religious individualism she resented some of their more strait-laced denunciations of the 'immorality' of European Romantics. In particular, she campaigned personally against Emerson's readiness to make moral judgements.

Goethe and his writings also tuned in with her own emotional needs. Entangled by the demands of her family, in the later 1830s Fuller formed a series of relationships, idealised in her own mind. Emerson wrote that '[she] wore this circle of friends, when I first knew her, as a necklace of diamonds about her neck'. This sentiment was echoed by Channing, also in the *Memoirs*: 'She was indeed, the Friend. This was her vocation'.[12]

Each of these relationships which involved a man (George Davis, Samuel Ward and Emerson himself) seemed doomed to disappointment and failure. It remains an interpretative task of some difficulty to recreate exactly their significance, given a context where, in Chevigny's words, 'the cult of friendship was part of the romanticism of the times'.[13] The female friendships which she cemented at this stage, with Caroline Sturgis and

11

Almira Barlow, with James Clarke's sister Sarah, and (until her marriage to Ward) with Anna Barker, the acknowledged beauty of the group, were, however, resilient and satisfying. Through Goethe they were even given a kind of philosophical warrant, as Fuller tried to prove with her translation of the correspondence between Goethe's young friend Bettina Brentano and her mentor Karoline von Günderode. Men were warier and less certain of how they could and should respond, as her relationship with Emerson and the transcendentalist circle demonstrates.

# Notes

1. *Memoirs of Margaret Fuller Ossoli*, ed. R. W. Emerson, W. H. Channing and J. F. Clarke, 3 vols., London: Richard Bentley, 1852 (hereafter *Memoirs*), I, p. 7.
2. Barbara Welter, 'The Cult of True Womanhood', in *Dimity Convictions: The American Woman in the Nineteenth Century*, Athens: Ohio University Press, 1976 (hereafter Welter, *Dimity Convictions*), pp. 21–41.
3. Paula Blanchard, *Margaret Fuller: From Transcendentalism to Revolution*, New York: Delacorte/Seymour Lawrence, 1978 (hereafter Blanchard), p. 3.
4. Thomas Wentworth Higginson, *Margaret Fuller Ossoli*, Boston: Greenwood Press, 1890 (hereafter Higginson), p. 22.
5. See Katherine Anthony, *Margaret Fuller: A Psychological Biography*, London: Jonathan Cape, 1922 (hereafter Anthony), p. 25; and Bell Gale Chevigny, *The Woman and the Myth: Margaret Fuller's Life and Writings*, Old Westbury, New York: Feminist Press, 1976 (hereafter Chevigny 1976a), pp. 19–21.
6. *Memoirs*, I, pp. 4–5, 8–11, 21.
7. Ibid, pp. 48–63.
8. Bell Gale Chevigny, 'Daughters Writing: Toward a Theory of Women's Biography', *Feminist Studies*, 9:1, Spring 1983 (hereafter Chevigny 1983), pp. 79–102.
9. Higginson, p. 34.
10. *Memoirs*, I, p. 201.
11. Chevigny 1976a, p. 174; compare the edited account in *Memoirs*, I, p. 236.
12. *Memoirs*, I, p. 284, II, p. 222.
13. Chevigny 1967a, p. 66.

# 2 Boston and the Transcendentalists

Ralph Waldo Emerson was, of course, the most formidable of Fuller's potential intellectual rivals. In 1836 he had published a modestly–sized book that proved a reasonable commercial success. As one of several manifestoes published by men who were beginning to style themselves 'transcendentalists', *Nature* heralded an attack of unprecedented scope on the orthodox ideas of Protestant New England.

The book begins with a complaint about the second-hand quality of the educated American's perception of the world.

> Our age is retrospective. It builds the sepulchres of the fathers. It writes biographies, history and criticism. The foregoing generations beheld God and nature face to face; we, through their eyes. Why should we also not enjoy an original relation to the universe? Why should not we have a poetry and philosophy of insight and not of tradition, and a religion by revelation to us, and not the history of theirs?

Then, in the first formal chapter, Emerson describes a radically alternative way of seeing, using as an example his experience on a country walk.

> Crossing a bare common, in snow puddles, at twilight, under clouded sky, without having in my thoughts any occurrence of special good fortune, I have enjoyed a perfect exhilaration. I am glad to the brink of fear. In the woods too, a man casts off his years, as the snake his slough, and at what period soever, is always a child. In the woods is perpetual youth. Within these plantations of God a decorum and sanctity reign, a perennial festival is dressed, and the guest sees not how he should tire of them in a thousand years. In the woods we return to reason and faith. There I feel that nothing can befall me in life, — no disgrace, no calamity (leaving me my eyes), which nature cannot repair. Standing on the bare ground, — my head bathed by the blithe air, and uplifted into infinite space, — all mean egotism vanishes. I become a transparent eyeball; I am

nothing; I see all; the currents of Universal Being circulate through me; I am part or parcel of God.

Although this final image embarrassed and amused some of Emerson's supporters (his friend Christopher Cranch drew a sketch of the author as an enormous eyeball, with two spindly legs) it has broad application as the centre of Emerson's transcendentalist epistemology. The claim is that an immediate, personal experience of the natural world brings the agent into an identity with the infinite and the Divine. The insight dissolves a number of traditional dualities; between the individual and the wider world, between concrete and spiritual experiences, and between 'natural' and 'revealed' religion.

In the remaining seven chapters of *Nature* implications of this doctrine are discussed. Nature is seen as having several distinct uses: as a 'commodity'; as the example of 'beauty'; as the inspiration of 'language' (which is presented as a symbolic scheme for recording the spiritual truths behind natural facts); and as an educative 'discipline', informing both the 'Understanding' (which deals with the true world of 'matter') and the 'Reason' (which elevates resulting perception to the plane of 'thought'). The stress is on man's participation in the world of spirit, ensured first of all by the necessity of the philosophy of idealism (which 'sees the world in God') and then by the operation of Spirit itself. '[Spirit], that is the Supreme Being, does not build up nature around us, but puts it forth through us.' The final chapter, 'Prospects', returns to the dichotomy Emerson has established between the 'Understanding' and 'Reason'. 'At present, man applies to nature but half of his force. He works in the world with his understanding alone.' Glimmers of the potential achievements of Reason are available, but further reorientation is required. 'The problem of restoring to the world original and eternal beauty, is solved by the redemption of the soul.'[1]

When Emerson published *Nature* it was approximately four years after he had resigned from the pastorate of the Second (Unitarian) Church of Boston, three years after the death of his first wife (whose legacy ensured his financial comfort for the rest of his life) and his first trip to Europe (during which he met Coleridge, Wordsworth, and Carlyle), and two years after he had moved to Concord and founded with Henry Thoreau (1817–62)

14

the loose association which its members liked to call the 'Transcendental Club'.

His later reputation has served to disguise the rather bizarre unorthodoxy he was proposing here. Emerson was attacking not only Calvinist (or Presbyterian-Congregationalist) orthodoxy, with its insistence on human depravity and the divine but selective origin of grace, but also the liberal Unitarian alternative that had grown out of it, with its reliance on the rational scientific confidence of the Enlightenment. To take a key issue over which the orthodox and liberal descendants of New England Puritans had fought — the nature of 'historical' Christianity, and the manner in which God revealed his truth through miracles or special providences — Emerson was declaring the debate irrelevant. God, the Universal Spirit, or what he was later to call the 'Oversoul', was not only working through man, he required man's participation. In the words of Murray Murphey, 'by identifying himself with the God within, man becomes a channel through which the Spirit works, and so, since nature is merely the spirit's imagery, he can rewrite it for himself'.[2]

This lack of respect for the preoccupations of the Establishment also underlay Emerson's next two famous forays. In the oration to the Phi Beta Kappa Society at Harvard in August 1837, entitled 'The American Scholar', Emerson castigated American higher education for its reliance on books and tradition rather than on the perception of nature available to the genuine scholar, the 'man thinking'. 'Nature' and 'Action' should combine to overcome the deleterious effects of 'the Mind of the Past'. 'Character', Emerson declared, 'is higher than intellect. Thinking is the function. Living is the functionary.' The duties of the Scholar 'may all be comprised in self-trust'. In the 'Divinity School Address', again by invitation to a group of Harvard students, in July 1838, he carried the battle into the heart of the Unitarian camp. The Church was denounced for its errors in the 'administration of Christianity', especially its neglect of 'the *person* of Jesus', its failure to explore the 'moral nature', and its 'unworthy' preaching. Again, salvation is seen in the individual, intuited moral sentiment. '[By] it is the universe made safe and habitable.' 'We have contrasted the Church and the Soul. In the soul, then, let the redemption be sought.' The reaction was confirmation for the Presbyterians in their view that Unitarianism led directly to heresy, and agony for the Unitarians as they were forced to find common ground with their old enemies against this new form of infidelity.[3]

Emerson's career as an essayist and lecturer was to last another forty years, but already most of the major features of his world view had been promulgated. Its twin pillars were the idealist conception of reality, and the emphasis on 'self-reliance', 'self-trust', or the confidence in the capacity of the individual soul to intuit its identity with the Divine. Technical doctrines which assisted the former included the belief in the 'correspondence' between spiritual and natural worlds (a long-standing idealist tenet) and a theory of 'compensation', which appeared at this stage to dismiss the element of evil or tragedy in the world by defining it (as in the Divinity School Address) merely as the absence of good. 'Self-reliance' meanwhile implied radical individualism (the importance of what Emerson was later to call 'the angle of vision' of each observer) and a new, romantic view of what was meant by Reason — not the scientific ratiocination of the Enlightenment, confined by Emerson to the 'understanding', but a higher order of intuitive insight. It also implied grandiose claims for the results of intuitive and spiritual participation. Emerson's *Journal* in October 1840 reports a dream in which the world appeared to him as an apple, which he proceeded to eat.

In March 1839 Fuller moved her family to Jamaica Plain in Boston, closer to the hub of this particular universe. By then she could fairly claim membership of the transcendentalist circle, although this was a fact which the more misogynous founders (including Emerson himself) found hard fully to accept. Her membership was based partly on philosophical affinity, on some specific and practical contributions, and on an emerging critical stance which foreshadowed her eventual break with the movement and its priorities. Weaving through all of these qualifications is the thread of her personal relationship with Emerson.

In 1840 Fuller recorded her own mystical experience, in language and with conclusions strongly reminiscent of *Nature*, but concluding with a note of disappointment: '[When] I consider that this will be nine years ago next November, I am astonished that I have not gone faster since; that I am not yet sufficiently purified to be taken back to God'. The episode took place in November 1831, after a Thanksgiving church service which she had attended reluctantly to please her father.

I paused beside a little stream, which I had envied in the merry fulness of its spring life. It was shrunken, voiceless, choked with withered leaves. I marvelled that it did not quite lose itself in the earth. There was no stay for me, and I went on and on, till I came to where the trees were thick about a little pool, dark and silent. I sat down there. I did not think; all was dark, and cold, and still. Suddenly the sun shone out with that transparent sweetness, like the last smile of a dying lover, which it will use when it has been unkind all a cold autumn day. And, even then, passed into my thought a beam from its true sun, from its native sphere, which has never since departed from me. I remembered how, a little child, I had stopped myself one day on the stairs, and asked, how came I here? How is it that I seem to be this Margaret Fuller? What does it mean? What shall I do about it? I remembered all the times and ways in which the same thought had returned. I saw how long it must be before the soul can learn to act under these limitations of time and space, and human nature; but I saw also, that it MUST do it, — that it must make all this false true, — and saw new and immortal plants in the garden of God, before it could return again. I saw there was no self; that selfishness was all folly, and the result of circumstance; that it was only because I thought self real that I suffered; that I had only to live in the idea of the ALL, and all was mine. This truth came to me and I received it unhesitatingly; so that I was for that hour taken up into God. In that true way most of the relations of earth seemed mere films, phenomena.[4]

This passage not only demonstrates affinities with Emerson's conversion experience but also points to future divergence. Fuller's religious commitments, although undoubtedly as deeply felt as Emerson's, at this stage lacked both the precision and the confidence of the latter's belief in a Universal Being. With hindsight, the tone of her surrender 'up into God' is deeply ambiguous. Similarly characteristic of Fuller's later writing are the suggestion of a desired sensual as well as intellectual fulfilment (the 'dying lover') and her determination to put the lesson of the experience to personal use. She continues by declaring, against all those real and imagined slights of her youth, 'my earthly pain at not being recognized never went deep after this hour'.

If statements like these emphasise services supplied to Fuller by the movement and its members, they were speedily and effectively repaid. Beyond her role as an intermittently acknowledged consultant on German Romanticism, Fuller made two major contributions to the public face of transcendentalism, the first indirect and the second direct.

In Boston she earned modest fame, and a little money, from her 'Conversations': discussion classes for women about grand moral and aesthetic questions, which ran, a little sporadically, from November 1839 until the final session in April 1844. In a long letter to Sophia Ripley she set out some of her intentions:

> . . . if my office were only to suggest topics, which would lead to conversation of a better sort than is usual at social meetings, and to turn back the current when digressing into personalities or commonplaces, so that what is valuable in the experience of each might be brought to bear upon all, I should think the object not unworthy of the effort.
>
> But my ambition goes much further. It is to pass in review the departments of thought and knowledge, and endeavour to place them in due relation to one another in our minds. To systematize thought, and give a precision and clearness in which our sex are so deficient, chiefly, I think, because they have so few inducements to test and classify what they receive. To ascertain what pursuits are best suited to us, in our time and state of society, and how we may make best use of our means for building up the life of thought upon the life of action.[5]

It is hard to estimate how successful she was. Men, including Emerson, were eventually allowed to join one series, and by all accounts wrecked it. Descriptions of the events by participants have been stitched together into a magnificent evocation of the occasion by Madeline Stern, emphasising the sense female participants had of being goaded into thinking systematically. But they also prompted satire and criticism for the pretentiousness of the themes (like that of 22 March 1841: 'What is Life?') and their ethereal quality.[6]

More short-lived was Fuller's editorship of *The Dial: a magazine for literature, philosophy and religion* from 1840 to 1842. *The Dial* was the transcendentalists' most sustained collaborative effort. It is no exaggeration to say that without Fuller, to whom the major figures turned almost by default as its editor for the first two years of its four-year life, it would never have started. Given the lack of discipline of the group it was a thankless task; it made no money, and by the time she handed it over, in exhaustion, to Emerson in July 1842 she had been easily the largest contributor.

Disappointed as she was by the enterprise at this stage, with hindsight the significance of her achievement stands out, not only in rigorously editing the more illustrious contributions (there are some delightfully tart exchanges with Emerson, and both Alcott and Thoreau suffered rejection) but in the directions established for her own work. These included not only examples of mature and original criticism, and a ground-breaking article on the art of criticism itself ('Short Essay on Critics'), but also the core of her most famous work in a lengthy essay appearing in July 1843: 'The Great Lawsuit: Man *versus* Men; Woman *versus* Women'.

By the early 1840s Fuller was beginning to produce serious and original work. Another important outcome was her travel book *Summer on the Lakes*, an account of a trip to Niagara Falls and west into Illinois, Wisconsin and Ohio with James Clarke and his sister Sarah in the summer of 1843. On one level this is another work in the transcendentalist genre of travel as self-culture and self-discovery (of which Thoreau's *A Week on the Concord and Merrimack Rivers*, 1849, is the archetype). Beyond this the book is noteworthy for an emerging strain of social criticism (about the lives of women on the frontier, and of treatment of the American Indian, for example) and the inclusion of a series of personal statements in rhetorical and allusive form.

One of these — the 'Mariana fable' (omitted by her brother from the second edition) — has been discussed above. Another is a dialogue between figures called 'Good Sense', 'Old Church', and 'Self-Poise', and the author herself as 'Free Hope'. As Chevigny and others have noted, 'Self-Poise' is Emerson, and here Fuller begins to mark her distance from him personally as well as with what she felt was represented by his transcendental spirit:

> You, Self-Poise, fill a priestly office. Could but a larger intelligence of the vocations of others, and a tender sympathy with their individual natures, be added, had you more of love, or more of apprehensive genius, (for either would give you the

needed expansion and delicacy), you would command my entire reverence. As it is, I must at times deny and oppose you, and so must others, for you tend, by your influence, to exclude us from our full, free life. We must be content when you censure, and rejoiced [sic] when you approve; always admonished to good by your whole being, and sometimes by your judgement.[7]

The 'sometimes' in the final sentence of the dialogue is a subtle wound. By the time of writing, the crisis in the relationship with Emerson (painstakingly reconstructed by modern scholars like Harry Warfel and Carl Strauch) was long past. Things had come to a head in the autumn of 1840, when Emerson finally retreated in the face of Fuller's pressing demand that he assist her in defining and developing their friendship. She wrote to him on 29 September demanding: 'But did you not ask for a "foe" in your friend? Did you not ask for a "large formidable nature?" But a beautiful foe, I am not yet, to you'. Like others before him, Emerson retreated. He wrote on 24 October:

There is a difference in our constitutions. We use a different rhetoric. It seems as if we had been born and bred in different nations. You say you understand me wholly. You cannot communicate yourself to me. I hear the words sometimes, but remain a stranger to your state of mind. Yet we are all the time a little nearer. I know you for a brave and beneficent woman, and mark with gladness your steadfast good-will to me. I see not how we can bear each other anything else than good-will, though we had sworn to the contrary. And now, what will you? the stars in Orion do not quarrel this night, but shine in peace in the old society. Are we not much better than they? Let us lie as we always have done, only ever better, I hope and richer. Speak to me of everything but myself, and I will endeavour to make an intelligible reply.

The effect of this rejection, for rejection it surely was, was compounded by the marriage of two of her closest friends Sam Ward and Anna Barker in the same month. It took some weeks for Fuller, who had pinned hopes for her type of friendship on each (she had probably been in love with Ward), and who was taken by surprise, to respond and congratulate them. Essentially

Emerson had given up, as possibly had Ward and Davis before him. The warmth of his previous response to her tutorials on Goethe, to her copies of and comments on works from the Boston Atheneum and especially her concern to define their relationship gave way to coolness and an eventual reconstruction of the relationship on an affectionate but less charged plateau. (Chevigny is, I believe, the only one of Fuller's biographers who speculates about how his wife Lidian may have reacted to all of this.)[8]

Nevertheless by 1844 and the publication of *Summer on the Lakes*, much of Fuller's ardour as well as her enthusiasm for the transcendentalist cause had waned. Another indicator of her growing estrangement was her reaction to life at Brook Farm, the transcendentalists' first and most sustained effort at a communal life. Created by George Ripley (1802–80), who had promised to publish her life of Goethe, and his wife Sophie Dana (an author in her own right), the experiment did not survive its attempted transformation in 1844 into a 'phalanx' of interconnected occupations along the lines recommended by the early French socialist Charles Fourier (1772–1837). After its eventual collapse in 1847, saddled with the debts, Ripley in fact was to succeed Fuller in her post on the *New York Tribune* and establish a major career as a literary critic, publisher and encyclopaedist. Fuller visited the commune at its height, attempted to establish her brother Lloyd there, and remarked self-importantly: 'I have found myself here in the amusing position of a conservative. Even so is it with Mr. R. There are too many young people in proportion to the others. I heard myself saying, with a grave air, "Play out the play, gentles." Thus, from generation to generation, rises and falls the wave'.[9]

To the surprise of many of her friends and her family, she accepted an invitation from Horace Greeley to move to New York and write for his *Tribune*. Before she took up her new post in December, Greeley encouraged her to take a holiday and work on a revision and expansion of 'The Great Lawsuit'. This was to become *Woman in the Nineteenth Century*.

# Notes

1. *The Collected Works of Ralph Waldo Emerson: Vol. 1 — Nature, Addresses and Lectures*, ed., Robert E. Spiller and Alfred R. Ferguson, Cambridge, Mass.: Harvard University Press, 1971 (hereafter Emerson, *Collected Works*), pp. 7, 10, 36, 38, 42–3.
2. Elizabeth Flower and Murray G. Murphey, *A History of Philosophy in America*, 2 vols., New York: G.P. Putnam's Sons, 1977, I, pp. 397–435, quotation p. 425.
3. Emerson, *Collected Works*, pp. 49–93.
4. *Memoirs*, I, pp. 183–5.
5. *Memoirs*, II, pp. 129–30; *The Letters of Margaret Fuller*, 5 vols., ed. Robert N. Hudspeth, Ithaca and London: Cornell University Press, 1983, (hereafter *Letters*), II, pp. 86–7.
6. Madeleine B. Stern, *The Life of Margaret Fuller*, New York: E.P. Dutton, 1942 (hereafter Stern), pp. 181–98.
7. Margaret Fuller Ossoli, *Summer on the Lakes,* ed. Arthur B. Fuller, New York: Haskell House, 1970 repr. of 2nd edn, 1856, (hereafter *Summer on the Lakes*), p. 75.
8. See Carl F. Strauch, '"Hatred's Swift Repulsions": Emerson, Margaret Fuller and Others', *Studies in Romanticism*, 7:2, Winter 1968, pp. 65–103; Harry R. Warfel, 'Margaret Fuller and Ralph Waldo Emerson' (1935), repr. in Joel Myerson (ed.), *Critical Essays on Margaret Fuller*, Boston: G.K. Hall, 1980 (hereafter Myerson (ed.), *Critical Essays*), pp. 161–77; *Letters*, II, pp. 80–1 and 90–1; Chevigny 1976a, p. 127.
9. *Memoirs*, II, p. 274.

# 3 New York and Europe, 1845–47

Fuller had been 'head-hunted' by Horace Greeley, one of *The Dial*'s small band of loyal subscribers, largely because of what she had written there. Greeley (1811–72) weaves an eccentric but influential path through the maze of nineteenth-century journalism and politics from his association with early anti-Jackson campaign weeklies (*The Jeffersonian*, 1838, and *The Log Cabin*, 1840), through authorship of a highly successful Civil War history (*The American Conflict*, 1864, 1866, which trailed a coat for the reconciliation wing of the postwar Republican party), to his final heroic failure in 1872 to defeat Ulysses S. Grant for the presidency on a combined Liberal-Republican and Democratic ticket. The *New York Tribune* was, however, his most lasting memorial. When Fuller joined the paper right at the end of 1844, it was barely three years old but had already achieved a wide circulation throughout the northern United States. Its platform was an idiosyncratic mixture of liberal social reform and economic protectionism.

Fuller joined the paper, in Miller's words as the 'first female member of the working press', a few months before the remarkable publishing success of *Woman in the Nineteenth Century* (1845) burst around her. The first edition of the book sold out within a week of its publication in February 1845, prompting a predictable series of reviews in the United States and Great Britain. Putting the almost uniformly hostile critical reception aside, publication of *Woman in the Nineteenth Century* was the most decisive step to date in Fuller's career. It drew attention to her work on the *Tribune* in a way that her limited-circulation essays in *The Dial* and other journals connected to the transcendentalists could never have achieved. A year later it, as much as any of the letters of introduction supplied by Emerson, opened up the *salons* of western Europe to her.

Greeley expected her to produce two or three articles a week on both literary and social topics (the two were frequently conflated, as a major device she came to use was the extended book review) and generally gave her space on the front page. The role she created within this framework was unprecedented, and not only because she was a woman. (Her predecessor, the American champion of Fourier, Albert Brisbane, 1809–90, had generally restricted his coverage to fairly doctrinaire social commentary.) In the space of the approximately 200 articles she wrote while in New York, Fuller extended the critical concerns she had developed on *The Dial* into a rudimentary theory of American exceptionalism, linked contemporary literature imaginatively with the social and economic context of its production, and raised questions about the life of the city which confirmed the prejudices of those who found *Woman in the Nineteenth Century* outspoken to the point of immorality.

In exploring these reactions it is important to remember that the agenda was almost more important than the content. Seekers of early traces of Fuller's socialism at this stage have generally been disappointed apart from the odd inclusion in the paper for 5 August 1845 of her translation of a brief commentary on political affairs in Paris from the correspondence of the *Deutsche Schnellpost* (one of her tasks was to monitor the foreign-language press). This referred to Marx and his major contemporary critics and ended with a quotation from Engels. Rather as she had done on *The Dial*, Fuller was concerned to acquaint her readers with developments in Europe, but at this stage no conclusions which could even broadly be called socialist are drawn. Allen characterises her chief concerns as 'individuals and private improvement', while Chevigny, suggesting that in the early 1840s she shared important elements of Emerson's temperamental conservatism, is cruelly accurate:

Liberal as her reportage was for the time, it was still eminently genteel muckraking: the Jew is subjected to age-old stereotyping, the poor to kindly pity. Her inexperience with social issues coupled with that questioned confidence in the authority of her own feelings made her naive or condescending in these pieces as often as she was moving and advanced.[1]

In several important respects Fuller was, however, making an intellectual break with the transcendentalists to accompany her physical removal from Boston and its more genteel hinterland. The literary criticism from this period, which she enlarged and published in 1846 as *Papers on Literature and Art*, builds on *The Dial*'s 'Essay on Critics' and particularises the American case. Her synoptic view of 'American Literature', built around a series of individual reviews from the *Tribune*, caused offence to those she felt overrated in their contribution (like Lowell) or those she ignored (like Poe) as well as pleasure to those she praised (including her later antagonist Nathaniel Hawthorne). American destiny, as she had hinted in *Summer on the Lakes* and *Woman in the Nineteenth Century* and would fully develop in her later writings from Europe, promised much and had so far underachieved.

> For it does not follow because many books are written by persons born in America that there exists an American literature. Books which imitate or represent the thoughts and life of Europe do not constitute an American literature. Before such can exist, an original idea must animate this nation and fresh currents of life must call into life fresh thoughts along its shores.[2]

The social and political analogues of the call for national leadership in the pages of the *Tribune* were rich and varied. Among the campaigns picked up by Fuller, and supported by Greeley, were: rehabilitation of female offenders (especially prostitutes), with enthusiastic articles on the Quaker Isaac Hopper's refuge for recently released prisoners on the Lower East Side as well as Eliza Farnham's revolutionary (and short-lived) programme of self-improvement for the female inmates of Sing Sing; opposition to the United States' expansionist war in Mexico (1846–8); anti-slavery (she was now firmly off the fence); anti-colonialism, including deep scepticism about the cultural impact of American exploration expeditions; and anti-nativism, including a staunch defence of Irish interests.

Limited though her analysis of several of these problems might appear with hindsight, coupled with the restricted range of her prescriptions for reform (many, in tune with the *Tribune*'s role as a campaigning paper, were thinly disguised appeals for charitable contributions), they all betokened a growing awareness of concrete conditions and their historical importance far removed from the abstract intellectualism of Emerson and his friends at Concord. Her paragraph on Emerson in the 'American Literature' essay is deeply respectful, but none the less contains the seeds of growing frustration with his suppression of the actual (in 1838, for example, he had agonised for a week in the pages of his journal before sending a letter to President Van Buren protesting about the forcible removal of Cherokee Indians).

> The Sage of Concord has a very different mind [from that of William Ellery Channing], in every thing except that he has the same disinterestedness and dignity of purpose, the same purity of spirit. He is a profound thinker. He is a man of ideas, and deals with causes rather than effects. His ideas are illustrated from a wide range of literary culture and refined observation, and embodied in a style whose melody and subtle fragrance enchant those who stand stupified before the thoughts themselves, because their utmost depths do not enable them to sound his shallows. His influence does not yet extend over a wide space; he is too far beyond his place and his time, to be felt at once or in full, but it searches deep, and yearly widens its inches. He is a harbinger of the better day.[3]

Socially as well as intellectually Fuller's life was also changing in character in New York. Higginson notes that she stopped writing diaries (the traditional transcendentalist work-bench) and slowed up on her letter writing. Initially she lived with the Greeleys in their riverside house in Turtle Bay. Here she mildly irritated Greeley who was an intermittent vegetarian, and a believer in more traditional kinds of self-discipline than the transcendentalists' endless self-scrutiny, with her addiction to tea and coffee, and her difficulty in rising in the morning. Her delight in children was also reflected in the intense relationship which she formed with the Greeleys' son 'Pickie'. Subsequently, when she moved out, ostensibly to be nearer the *Tribune* offices, although she continued to do most of her work at home, she engaged in the social life of the city with a zest it would have been hard to predict from her life in the family homes in Groton and Boston.[4]

During the spring and early summer of 1845 Fuller enjoyed a strange, almost certainly unconsummated affair with a young German businessman called James Nathan. Nathan has had a bad press with Fuller's biographers, not least because of his actions in keeping her letters after the affair was over (these were eventually published in 1903, after a long rearguard action by her family, as *Love-Letters of Margaret Fuller*). Chevigny, for example, calls him a 'deft social climber'. For all the more peculiar features of their relationship — it seems, for example, that he enlisted Fuller's help in dealing with the break-up of a previous affair — it is clear that she was conventionally in love. She defied the Greeleys to see him (they trysted in various friends' houses in New York) and the relationship survived (temporarily) a crisis when he apparently misunderstood and took literally one of her more metaphysical advances:

Are you my guardian to domesticate me in the body, and attach it more firmly to earth? Long it seemed, that it was only my destiny to say a few words to my youth's companions and then depart. I hang highly as an air-plant. Am I to be rooted on earth, ah! Choose for me a good soil and a sunny place, that I may be a green shelter to the weary and bear fruit enough for staying.[5]

Chevigny sees Fuller's adoption of a starkly conventional feminine role in the affair, subjugating her independence and dreaming of motherhood ('Perhaps it is, that I was not enough a child at the right time, and am now too childish; but will you not have patience with that?'), as possibly an 'experiment', succeeding a different kind of experiment with Emerson. If this was the case it none the less remained true that Fuller did not give up after Nathan's return to Europe in June 1845. Perry Miller suggests mischievously that he 'fled for his life'. She lavished affection on the Newfoundland puppy (Josey) he left her, assisted Nathan in getting his travel notes published (in the *Tribune* and elsewhere), and did not abandon all hope of the friendship blossoming until after she learned (in England in 1846) of his engagement to another.[6]

By her thirty-sixth year Fuller had achieved a career that brought her fame and respect as well as notoriety, and a relatively secure social situation in the liberal wing of social thinkers and reformers in New York. She was also feeling stronger than at any previous time in her adult life; the famous Dr Leger, at whose house she occasionally met Nathan, had made some progress in alleviating pain from the curvature of her spine. It was from here that she embarked in August 1846, as companion to Quaker friends of the Greeleys, Marcus and Rebecca Spring and their son Eddie, on the first leg of what was intended to be a European grand tour. This was the trip her father had promised her and had never been able to provide, and which had been blocked by his brother Abraham as executor of the will. Now she was financing it herself, by loans from her friends and colleagues, but also by a contract with Greeley to report directly on the condition of Europe for the *Tribune*.

\* \* \*

Notwithstanding her ambiguous role as an informal employee of the Springs, Fuller arrived in Liverpool in late 1847 as considerably more of a celebrity. Her reputation as editor of *The Dial* and author of *Woman in the Nineteenth Century* and *Papers on Literature and Art*, her foreign correspondence for the *Tribune*, in addition to her friendship with figures like Harriet Martineau and letters of introduction like that supplied to Carlyle by Emerson, provided an *entrée* that her employers were keen to share. Not that Fuller was content for her grand tour to become a sequence of visits to *salons*; rather she succeeded in Britain and France, as in New York, in combining intellectual pursuits with a rigorous programme of social and political investigation.

The latter, according to Chevigny, 'shocked her into class awareness'. Many of Fuller's expeditions were recapitulations of her experience in New York — accounts of urban poverty in Manchester and Glasgow, penal reform in Pentonville, sweated labour in Lyons, educational reform, and female self-improvement — and she spiced her *Tribune* dispatches with comparative judgements. She also began to enlarge on the theories of national destiny which she had hinted at in the essay on American literature and set out explicitly in a *Tribune* column of 1 January 1846:

> Forms come and go, but principles are developed and displayed more and more. The caldron simmers, and so great is the fire that we expect it soon to boil over, and new fates appear for Europe.
> Spain is dying by inches; England shows symptoms of having passed her meridian; Austria has taken opium, but she must awake ere long; France is in an uneasy dream — she knows she has been very sick, has had terrible remedies admin-

istered and ought to be getting thoroughly well, which she is not. . . .

No power is in the ascending course except the Russian; and that has such a condensation of brute force, animated by despotic will, that it seems sometimes as if it might by and by stride across Europe and face us across the water. Then would be opposed to me rather the two extremes of Autocracy and Democracy, and a trial of strength would ensue between the two principles more grand and full than any ever seen on this planet, and of which the result must be to bind mankind by one chair of conviction.[7]

Soon her social calendar began to reflect this merging of literary and political interests. The trip did not begin propitiously. The first visit, to Harriet Martineau in Ambleside, was by all accounts other than Fuller's (she recommenced a diary for this early part of the trip) an edgy affair. Martineau's *Society in America* (1836) had been scathing about the political quiescence of many of Fuller's friends (especially Bronson Alcott). Fuller, for her part, had received it unfavourably, suggesting that Martineau failed to recognise the true moral worth of transcendentalism. There was also some tension over what Martineau described as Fuller's haughty manner, and her apparent attempt to monopolise Martineau's medical guru, the mesmerist Henry Atkinson. A brief visit to the ageing William Wordsworth was more satisfactory.[8]

Then, as the party moved on to Scotland, Fuller suffered two experiences from which her mood rebounded in an unpredictably positive way. The first was the resolution of the affair with Nathan, who finally responded to her letters planning to visit him in Germany by writing and telling her of his engagement. After a brief period of silence Fuller responded through an intermediary, that she was 'too much involved in the routine of visiting and receiving visitors to allow her mind a moment's repose to reply'.[9] The second was an alarming night spent on Ben Lomond after she had lost Marcus Spring on a walk to the summit. The outcome, as she characteristically recorded it in terms of a personal lesson, was anything but a further transcendentalist experience of the infinite. For Fuller it resulted in a 'never-to-be-forgotten presentation of stern, severe realities'.[10]

In London she finally met Carlyle, Emerson's closest English friend, and apparently made more of an impression on him than he on her, although she wrote admiringly about the patience and forbearance of his wife Jane. Through the Carlyles she also met Giuseppe Mazzini for whose ideas she felt an instant affinity. Mazzini was now in his fifteenth year of exile and struck a romantic figure, with his daily apparel of mourning for the suppressed Italian nation, his fund-raising circuit through the British intelligentsia, and his school for Italian immigrants. Fuller addressed the school, later conspired with the Springs to assist Mazzini to obtain papers to re-enter Italy illegally, and began a dialogue about idealism and political progress that was to be profound importance through tha last three years of her life.

In November 1846 the group moved on to Paris, and basked again in some of the limelight of Fuller's fame. The working pattern for Fuller was the same: observation of social and political affairs (comparing the English 'John Bull' with the French, 'who can cheat you pleasantly, and move with grace in the devious and slippery path') and visiting local luminaries. As she remarked on French politics, 'the French have a truly Greek vivacity; they cannot endure to be bored'.[11] She learned about Fourierite socialism at its source, meeting his disciple Victor-Prosper Considérant, and finding it a much more vital set of ideas in the aftermath of the French Revolution than Ripley and Greeley had been able to persuade her.

There were also the leading literary lights to visit, including the spokesmen of the revolutionary tradition like Pierre Jean de Béranger and Robert de Lamenais. Two further encounters were particularly important, one for reviewing and modifying a long-standing role model, the other for providing the kind of male friend she now saw Emerson might have become had he persevered.

Fuller had been ambivalent in her final estimate of George Sand in *Woman in the Nineteenth Century*, wondering if her example of courage and independence had been bought at too great a price in terms of mockery of contemporary morals. Her life style had made it easy for critics to dismiss her ideas. When they met finally in early 1847 difficulties in communication were soon overcome (Fuller regretted throughout the trip that she had learned French as a written and not a spoken language) and her doubts faded away. She wrote to her friend Elizabeth Hoar in terms which prefigure in some important respects her later estimate of her own strengths and weakness.

> She has that purity in her soul, for she knows well how to love and prize its beauty; but she herself is quite another sort of person. She needs no defence, but only to be understood, for she has bravely acted out her nature, and always with good intentions. She might have loved one man permanently, if she could have found one contemporary with her who could interest and command her throughout her range; but there was hardly a possibility of that, for such a person.[12]

In time Adam Mickiewicz, the Polish poet and nationalist in exile, was to become Fuller's most frank personal confessor. They met shortly before she and the Springs left for Italy in February of 1847, and formed a relationship based on a shared set of personal sensibilities that was to be at least as important during her Italian adventure as her political affinities with Mazzini. Mickiewicz, in short, urged her to pursue personal and sexual fulfilment in addition to her more metaphysical projects ('for you the first step of your deliverance . . . is to know whether you are to be permitted to remain a virgin'). She wrote to Emerson in ironic terms: 'I found in him the man I had long wished to see, with the intellect and passions in due proportion for a full and healthy human being, with a soul constantly inspiring'.[13]

It is perhaps useful to speculate about Fuller's personal state when she and the Springs arrived in Rome in the spring of 1847, where she was to spend the rest of her working life. Her first dispatch to the *Tribune*, in May 1847, anticipated a long attachment to the country and its people.

> Yet I find that it is quite out of the question to know Italy; to say anything of her that is full and sweet, so as to convey any idea of her spirit, without long residence, and residence in the districts untouched by the scorch and dust of foreign invasion (the invasion of the *dilletanti* I mean), and without an intimacy of feeling or abandonment to the spirit of the place, impossible to most Americans.[14]

Chevigny and others have pointed to the effect of distance from the United States on both her growing political sophistication and her personal maturity. Chevigny puts the point bluntly: 'Europe was offering her two crucial sensations America never did: the shock of class consciousness and warm bath of personal (and implicitly physical) self-acceptance'.[15]

In St Peter's Cathedral, after Mass on Easter Sunday, Fuller made another European friend. The 26-year-old Giovanni Angelo Ossoli, fourth son of a minor aristocratic family with strong connections with the papal hierarchy, found her separated from the Springs and escorted her on foot back to her lodgings. As they walked he began to tell her about his family, his life and his republican sympathies. She was able to reciprocate by talking of Mazzini. By the time she and the Springs left in June for a tour of northern Italy and Switzerland her European tour had taken on some new dimensions, personal and political.[16]

# Notes

1. Margaret Vanderhaar Allen, *The Achievement of Margaret Fuller*, University Park and London: Penn State U. Press, 1979 (hereafter Allen 1979), p. 126; Chevigny 1976a, pp. 283, 291, 294.
2. S. Margaret Fuller, *Papers on Literature and Art*, 2 vols., London: Wiley & Putnam, 1846 (hereafter *Papers on Literature and Art*), II, pp. 122–59.
3. Ibid, p. 128.
4. Higginson, pp. 209–11.
5. *Love-Letters of Margaret Fuller 1845–46*, introd. Julia Ward Howe, London, 1903 (hereafter *Love-Letters*), p. 21.
6. Chevigny 1976a, pp. 80–1, 133–5; Perry Miller (ed.), *Margaret Fuller: American Romantic. A Selection from her Writings and Correspondence*, Ithaca: Cornell U. Press, 1963 (hereafter Miller (ed.), *Margaret Fuller*), p. 202.
7. Margaret Fuller Ossoli, *Life Without and Life Within; or, Reviews, Narratives, Essays, and Poems*, ed. Arthur B. Fuller, Upper Saddle River, NJ: Literature House/Gregg Press repr. of 1860 edn., 1970 (hereafter *Life Without and Life Within*), pp. 212–13.
8. Higginson, pp. 220–5; Blanchard, p. 249.
9. *Love-Letters*, pp. 187–9.
10. *Memoirs*, III, p. 91.
11. Margaret Fuller Ossoli, *At Home and Abroad, or Things and Thoughts in America and Europe*, ed. Arthur B. Fuller, Port Washington and London: Kennikat Press repr. of 1856 edn, 1971 (hereafter *At Home and Abroad*), pp. 170, 208; Chevigny 1976a, pp. 355–6.

12. *Memoirs*, III, p. 115.
13. See ibid, p. 129; Chevigny 1976a, p. 350.
14. *At Home and Abroad*, p. 220.
15. Chevigny 1976a, p. 298.
16. Joseph Jay Deiss, *The Roman Years of Margaret Fuller: A Biography*, New York: Thomas Crowell, 1969 (hereafter Deiss), pp. 56–7.

# 4 The Roman Revolution

The Italian states in 1847 were divided and, under the terms of the Congress of Vienna, which had marked the end of the Napoleonic Wars, dominated by foreign powers, principally Austria. Austrian hegemony was direct in most of the northern states, indirect in others like Tuscany, and similarly assured by family ties in Naples in the south. The central Papal States had a kind of spurious independence under the Vatican, as did the kingdom of Piedmont (Sardinia) in the northwest. Piedmont, under Charles Albert of the House of Savoy, had a liberal and nationalist reputation and was the home of Count Camillo Cavour, the eventual architect of Italian unification. However, Charles Albert had been responsible for suppressing both the early rising of the Carbonari and the 'Young Italy' movement of Mazzini.

Liberal hopes for a settlement of Italian political problems were focussed on the Papacy, especially after the election of Pius IX in June 1846 to succeed the authoritarian Gregory XVI. A series of reforms and gestures to constitutional reform culminated in May 1847 with the announcement of a representative assembly, celebrated in a huge torchlight procession down the Corso, which Fuller reported back to her *Tribune* readers.

Nothing could seem more limited than this improvement, but it was a great measure for Rome. At night the Corso in which we live was illuminated, and many thousands passed through it in a torch-bearing procession. I saw them first assembled in the Piazza del Popolo turning around its fountain a great circle of fire. Then, as a river of fire, they streamed slowly through the Corso, on their way to the Quirinal to thank the Pope, upbearing a banner on which the edict was printed. The stream of fire advanced slowly, with a perpetual surge-like sound of voices; the torches flashed on the anointed Italian faces. I have never seen anything finer. Ascending the Quirinal they made it a mount of light. Bengal fires were thrown up, which cast their red and white light on the noble Greek figures of men and horses that reign over it. The Pope appeared on his balcony; the crowd shouted three vivas; he extended his arms;

the crowd fell on their knees and received his benediction; he retired, and the torches were extinguished, and the multitude dispersed in an instant.[1]

Hopes seemed high for the spread of a kind of democratic liberalism throughout the region, as urged by the priest Abbé Vicenzo Gioberti from exile. Fuller, who recognised Gioberti as one of the obstacles to Mazzini's achievement of his aims, was sceptical.

During the momentous year of 1848 any prospect of gradualist reform fell apart as the Italian states, inspired by the French uprising of February against Louis Philippe, rebelled in a superficially coordinated manner against the Austrians. Sicily and Naples began the sequence, followed by constitutional reform in Piedmont and Tuscany, a Milanese tax revolt, and a proclamation of independence in Venice. Charles Albert, with equivocal support from the Pope, seized his chance and declared war against Austria in March.

Events through the next sixteen months were structured by the working out of these 'revolutions' and the reactions to them by the Austrians and French. By April 1848 the Pope had separated himself from Charles Albert and provoked a revolution against his own authority. Finally in November, after the brutal murder of his unpopular minister Pellegrino Rossi (reported for the *Tribune* by Fuller on the eye-witness evidence of her landlady), he was forced to flee to Naples. Fuller's judgement was significantly subjective.

I believe he really thinks now the Progress movement tends to anarchy, blood, and all that looked worst in the first French revolution. However that may be, I cannot forgive him some of the circumstances of this flight. To fly to Naples; to throw himself in the arms of the bombarding monarch, blessing him and thanking his soldiery for preserving that part of Italy from anarchy; to protest that all his promises at Rome were null and void, when he thought himself in safety to choose a commission for governing in his absence, composed of men of princely blood, but as to character so null that everybody laughed, and said he chose those who could best be spared if they were killed; (but they all ran away directly;) when Rome was thus left without any government, to refuse to see any deputation,

35

even the Senator of Rome, whom he had so gladly sanctioned, — these are the acts either of a fool or a foe. They are not his acts, to be sure, but he is responsible; he lets them stand as such in the face of the world, and weeps and prays for their success.

No more of this! His day is over. He has been made, it seems unconsciously, an instrument of good his regrets cannot destroy.[2]


Early in the new year (1849) Charles Albert's defeat resulted in his abdication and nationalist efforts became focused on Rome, where Mazzini had now arrived to rally his forces. The Roman Republic was proclaimed in February and Fuller used the columns of the *Tribune* to appeal for American help.

How I wish my country would show some noble sympathy when an experience so like her own is going on. Politically she cannot interfere; but formerly, when Greece and Poland were struggling, they were at least aided by private contribution. Italy, nationally so rich, but long racked and impoverished by her oppressors, greatly needs money to arm and clothe her troops. Some token of sympathy, too, from America would be so welcome to her now. If there were a circle of persons inclined to trust such to me, I might venture to promise the trust should be used to the advantage of Italy. It would make me proud to have my country show a religious faith in the progress of ideas, and make some small sacrifice of its own great resources in aid of a sister cause, now.[3]


Rome was by now also the target of the counter-revolution. The Pope had been forced into the arms of the Austrians, who enlisted Neopolitan, Spanish and, as Fuller had predicted (more accurately than Mazzini who had higher hopes of Louis Napoleon — a former supporter of the Carbonari), French help to suppress the Republic. It was eventually the French, arriving by sea, who laid siege to Rome and, after a heroic defence inspired not only by Mazzini but also by the remarkable irregular forces led by Guiseppe Garibaldi, defeated the republicans at the end of June.

Against this dramatic backcloth Fuller's role shifted subtly but inexorably from observer to participant. In October 1847 she had left the Springs in northern Italy, despite the fact that their next destination was Germany, the land of Goethe (which she never saw). Returning to Rome she set herself up in an apartment on the Via del Corso, carefully marshalled her limited finances, and embarked on an intensive programme of research and writing about the events around her. Paula Blanchard describes her circumstances:

> She lived very frugally. In September a letter of credit for $500 had arrived from [her brother] Richard. Soon afterward came a letter from Horace Greeley telling her to draw against the *Tribune* when she needed money. Her share of Uncle Abraham's estate [on which she had been banking to provide her independence] turned out to be less than $1,000 of which she already owed several hundred to Marcus Spring. She decided to try to make $400 last for six months, living in one room and subsisting mostly on fruit, bread and wine. . . . Her economical living quarters had the advantage of privacy, since they gave her a plausible excuse for seeing visitors only on Monday evenings.[4]

By this time Ossoli was her lover, and shortly to throw in his lot finally with the republican movement. On 15 November he risked the antagonism of his family (and disinheritance) by joining the Civil Guard.

In addition to Ossoli, her circle of friends (but not her correspondents) was limited. It included the Marchesa Constanza Arconati Visconti, recently returned from exile with her husband to Florence, where Fuller had first met her earlier in the year. Arconati, who had introduced Fuller to several of the leading liberal actors on the political scene, continued a regular correspondence with her in Rome and occasionally lent her money. Fuller came to rely on her for testing of both personal and political judgements.

Of the many Americans in Rome, few became close to Fuller. She came to mistrust their patronising attitude to the political scene and casual assumption of national superiority, and contributed a devastating typology of Americans in exile to the *Tribune*.

> There are three species. First, the servile American, — a being utterly shallow, thoughtless, worthless. He comes abroad to

spend his money and indulge his tastes. His object in Europe is to have fashionable clothes, good foreign cookery, to know some titled persons, and furnish himself with coffee-house gossip, by retailing which among those less travelled and as uninformed as himself he can win importance at home. . . .

Then there is the conceited American, instructively bristling and proud of — he knows not what. He does not see, not he, that the history of Humanity for many centuries is likely to have produced results it requires some training, some devotion, to appreciate and profit by. With his great clumsy hands, only fitted to work on a steam-engine, he seizes the old Cremona violin, makes it shriek with anguish in his grasp, and then declares he thought it was all humbug before he came, and now he knows it; that there is not really any music in these old things; that the frogs in one of our swamps make much finer, for they are young and alive . . . this is Jonathan in the sprawling state, the booby truant, not yet aspiring enough to be a good school-boy. Yet in his folly there is reason; add thoughts and culture to his independence, and he will be a man of might: he is not a creature without hope, like the thick-skinned dandy of the class first specified.

The artistes form a class by themselves. Yet among them, though seeking special aims by special means, may also be found the lineaments of these two classes, as well as of the third, of which I am now to speak.

This is that of the thinking American, — a man who, recognizing the immense advantage of being born to a new world and in a virgin soil, yet does not wish one seed from the past to be lost. He is anxious to gather and carry back with him every plant that will bear a new climate and a new culture.[5]

Some Americans met her stern test. After an uncertain beginning she did become close to the sculptor William Wetmore Story and his wife Emelyn, and, later came to admire and rely on the official US envoy Lewis Cass.

Her writing at this time grew in perception and authority. Sensing the needs of an American audience for an explanation not only of the complexity of events in the European political cauldron she had predicted for them before leaving, but also of their significance, she acknowledged belatedly the discovery of a vocation. As she wrote to Emerson in December 1847:

I find how true was the lure that always drew me to Europe. It was no false instinct that said I might find here an atmosphere to develop me in ways I need. Had I only come ten years earlier! Now my life must be a failure, so much strength had been wasted on abstractions which only came because I grew not in the right soil.

The elegiac tone of this extract (a voice which she often assumed for Emerson) should not mislead us about the satisfaction Fuller was drawing from her work. To another correspondent of increasing importance in the last two years of her life, her mother, she was able, almost simultaneously, to write: 'My life at Rome is thus far all I hoped. I have not been so well since I was a child, nor so happy ever, as during the last six weeks'. To her brother Richard she had written in October: 'I find myself so happy here, alone and free'.[6]

For Chevigny, Fuller had by this time achieved a perspective on American affairs that had always eluded her at home. She quotes at length the *Tribune* dispatch of May 1848:

My friends write to urge my return: they talk of our country as the land of the future. It is so, but that spirit which made it all it is of value in my eyes, which gave all of hope with which I can sympathize for the future, is more alive here at present than in America. My country is at present spoiled by prosperity, stupid with the lust of gain, soiled by crime in its willing perpetuation of slavery, shamed by an unjust war, noble sentiment much forgotten even by individuals, the airs of politicians selfish or petty, the literature frivolous and venal. In Europe, amid the teachings of adversity, a nobler spirit is struggling — a spirit which cheers and animates mine. I hear earnest words of pure faith and love. I see deeds of brotherhood. This is what makes my America. I do not deeply distrust my country. She is not dead, but in my time she sleepeth, and the spirit of our fathers flows no more, but lies buried beneath the ashes. It will not be so long: bodies cannot live when the soul gets too overgrown with gluttony and falsehood.[7]

Fuller's commitments were by this stage not only to the democratic republicanism of her friends but also to social groups oppressed by the current regimes. Earlier in the same dispatch she had written: 'The responsibility of events now lies wholly with the people, and that wave of thought which has begun to pervade them. . . . In Rome there is now no anchor except the good sense of the people'.[8]

Her feminism remained, but became allied to a form of socialism which saw in the liberation of the economically downtrodden more than the release of 'humanity' demanded by Mazzini. Although it is highly unlikely that she read the *Communist Manifesto*, her reactions to the French revolution of February 1848, and her observation of the true heroes of the siege, show significant progress beyond the sentimental, cooperative Fourierism to which she had been introduced by Ripley and Greeley. After the failure of the Republic she had no hesitancy about describing herself to the Springs as an 'enthusiastic Socialist' or declaring her colours to the *Tribune* readers: 'Young Europe will know next time that there is no possible compromise between her and the old'.[9]

The association between this evidence of political liberation and Fuller's personal life from the autumn of 1847 has bedevilled Fuller scholarship in ways which I discuss further below. Briefly, it is all too easy, as Barbara Welter warns, for us to see her as a Jamesian heroine ('a little too old for Daisy Miller, a little dry for Isabel Archer').[10]

Older accounts which see her falling in love immediately and unreservedly with both Ossoli and his cause have been undermined by detailed detective work. Chevigny has discovered a passionate correspondence with the American painter Thomas Hicks (who later painted a miniature of her during the siege, and refused to part with it, or their letters) dating from the period between her first meeting with Ossoli and her resumption of travel with the Springs. Chevigny also speculates about her relationship with the Milanese radical Guerrieri later that summer, bracketted together with Hicks in a letter to Emerson of September 1847 as 'minds that would interest you greatly'.[11]

By early 1848, however, her relationship with Ossoli was secure. The dispute about when, and if at all they were married rages on, inspired by her retrospective need to protect her lover and son and the Victorian sensibilities of her literary executors. Madeline Stern has assembled the evidence as convincingly as it can be, although many remain sceptical, noting the very limited range of occasions on which she was prepared to call Ossoli her husband.[12]

Her pregnancy, discovered early in the year, however, threatened not only her life (she was thirty-seven years old) but also her new-found professional independence. From late May she was compelled to leave Rome and found herself in lodgings, first in Aquila and then in Rieti. In this temporary exile she relied on Ossoli for moral support, for supplying her with materials for a projected history of the Roman struggle (now taking firm shape in her mind), and for manipulation of their complex financial affairs. He was able to visit her occasionally and was in Rieti on 5 September 1848 when their son Angelino (Nino) was born.

Ossoli's return soon after, and the legal complexities of baptism and vaccination against smallpox as an epidemic swirled around Rieti, have left a correspondence touching in its revelation of their mutual dependence as well as Fuller's growing satisfaction in watching her baby grow. In November, however, as political events and financial exigencies pressed, she was forced to leave Angelino in Rieti and returned herself, to an apartment in the Piazza Barberini, just in time to report the murder of Rossi.

From this point, except for a brief spell in Rieti in early March 1849, her practical energies were absorbed in Rome. For the duration of the siege she was appointed by the legendary Princess Cristina Belgioioso (like Arconati, who introduced them, a returned exile, although one with a considerably more flamboyant life style) as director of a republican hospital, the Fate Bene Fratelli, on an island in the Tiber.

It is hard to picture the pressures Fuller endured for the next three months, receiving demands for money from Angelino's nurse in Rieti, assisting the exhausted Ossoli, advising Mazzini, and writing her dispatches. Astonishingly the quality of her work for the *Tribune* during this period and the quantity of her correspondence hardly abated. The journalism was by now unashamedly partisan. As she wrote for the *Tribune* on 27 May 1849:

The struggle is now fairly, thoroughly commenced between the principle of democracy and the old powers, no longer legitimate. That struggle may last fifty years, and the earth be watered with the blood and tears of more than one generation, but the result is same. All Europe, including Great Britain,

41

where the most bitter resistance of all will be made, is to be under republican government in the next century.[13]

Meanwhile her correspondents were charged with reading hidden meaning into her personal news. She wrote to Emerson on 10 June reporting on the bombardment of Rome and its effect upon her patients, before issuing the following plea:

> Should I never return, and sometimes I despair of doing so, it seems so far off — so difficult, I am caught in such a net of ties here, — if ever you know of my life here, I think you will only wonder at the constancy with which I have sustained myself, — the degree of profit to which, amid great difficulties, I have put the time, — at least in the way of observation. Meanwhile, love me all you can. Let me feel that, amid the fearful agitations of the world, there are pure hands, with healthful, even pulse, stretched out toward me, if I claim their grasp.[14]

The night before the final defeat she spent with Ossoli at his post, having made elaborate and deceptive arrangements with her American friends for care of Angelino, fully expecting to be killed.

After the French entry into Rome on 4 July, Fuller worked for a few more days securing among other things official American assistance for Mazzini and other republican leaders (whom the French seemed curiously reluctant to arrest) and returned to Rieti with Ossoli. Angelino they found ill and almost starving, as the family with whom they had left him had given up prospect of their return. Of all the dilemmas her life alone had presented her, and which she had overcome, none seemed to have prepared her for what the family now faced together.

\* \* \*

Fuller's immediate reaction to the defeat of the Roman Republic was one of despair. In a letter of 8 July 1849 to her brother Richard she wrote: 'Private hopes of mine are fallen with the hopes of Italy. I have played for a new stake and lost it. Life looks too difficult'.[15]

As the Ossolis moved on from Rieti to Florence, and a temporarily settled social life which included former republican allies as well as expatriates such as the Storys and the Brownings, the pain

42

of defeat came to be tempered by the satisfaction of a first experience of normal family life. Fuller's letters during the summer of 1849, extensively extracted in the *Memoirs*, are a curious mixture of resentment and fear of the Austrian and French conquerers, half-hearted attempts to predict the eventual success of republican revolution, concern at her own weariness and state of mind, and unalloyed delight in the growing-up of Nino and the attentions of Ossoli. This, for example, is the collage made by the editors to demonstrate her state of mind after the recovery of Angelino:

> I shall never again . . . be perfectly, be religiously generous, so terribly do I need for myself the love I have given to other sufferers. When you read this, I hope your heart will be happy; for I still like to know that others are happy, it consoles me. . . . O God! help me, is all my cry. Yet I have so little faith in the Paternal love I need, so ruthless or so negligent seems the government of this earth. I feel calm, yet sternly towards Fate. This last plot against me has been so cruelly, cunningly wrought that I shall never acquiesce. I submit, because useless resistance is degrading, but I demand an explanation. I see that it is probable I shall never receive one while I live here, and suppose I can bear the rest of the suspense, since I have comprehended all its difficulties in the first moments. Meanwhile, I live day by day, but not on manna. . . . I have been the object of great love for the noble and the humble; I have felt it towards both. Yet I am *tired out*, — tired of thinking and hoping, — tired of seeing men err and bleed. I take interest in some plans, — Socialism, for instance, — but the interest is as shallow as the plans. These are needed, are even good: but man will still blunder and weep, as he has done for so many thousand years.[16]

The other growing cloud over the family was, of course, the problem of ensuring their social security and economic independence. Through the remainder of 1849 and into 1850 Fuller continued the process of progressive revelation of her circumstances and her motives to friends and relations which she had begun during the uprisings of early 1849 and continued through the siege. Then she had partially confessed her situation, and attempted to ensure the safety of Angelino, with the help of Emelyn Story, Hicks, and Lewis Cass. With each of these she left packets of letters and papers which have only served further to confuse the debate about her marriage.

Her initial transatlantic explanations came in letters to women friends (particularly Caroline Sturgis) and most significantly her mother to whom she tried to explain Ossoli's character:

> He is not in any respect such a person as people in general would expect to find with me. He had no instructor except an old priest, who entirely neglected his education; and of all that is contained in books he is absolutely ignorant, and he has no enthusiasm of character. On the other hand, he has excellent practical sense; has been a judicious observer of all that passed before his eyes; has a nice sense of duty, which, in its unfailing, minute activity, may put most enthusiasts to shame; a very sweet temper, and great native refinement. His love for me has been unswerving and most tender. I have never suffered a pain that he could relieve. His devotion, when I am ill, is to be compared only with yours. His delicacy in trifles, his sweet domestic graces, remind me of E[ugene]. In him I have found a home, and one that interferes with no tie. Amid many ills and cares, we have had much joy together, in the sympathy with natural beauty, — with our child, — with all that is innocent and sweet.
>
> I do not know whether he will always love me so well, for I am the elder, and the difference will become, in a few years, more perceptible than now. But life is so uncertain, and it is so necessary to take good things with their limitations, that I have not thought it worth while to calculate too curiously.
>
> However my other friends may feel, I am sure that *you* will love him very much, and that he will love you no less. Could we all live together on a moderate income, you would find peace with us.[17]

She was delighted by a loving and uncomplicated response:

> No words of mine could give you any idea of the effect your communication of having become wife and mother made upon me. I had thought that nothing could ever move the depths of my spirit as this did. I have had time for calm reflection, and assure you that fervent thankfulness has come out of all this thought, that I should have suffered tortures to have known that you were to become a mother and I so far from you. . . .You are the only one who could judge of what could

make you so happy. . . . If he continues to make you happy, he will be very dear to me.[18]

Without a trace of self-pity on this score, Fuller appreciated that the future of her husband and son rested with her and her decisions, and began to estimate her options. She looked to her writing, and particularly to her projected book on the Roman Revolution, to provide their livelihood, and began to make discreet enquiries about its publication in Britain and the United States. At this stage the worst of her fears were realised, as her friends, anticipating that she had brought scandal upon herself and them, began to warn about the social consequences of her return. To Rebecca Spring she wrote pugnaciously:

I am sure your affection for me will prompt you to add, that you feel confident whatever I have done has been in a good spirit, and not contrary to my ideas of right. For the rest you will not admit for me, — as I do not for myself, — the right of the social inquisition of the United States to know all the details of my affairs. If my mother is content; if Ossoli and I are content; if our child, when grown up shall be content; that is enough. You and I know enough of the United States to be sure that many persons there will blame whatever is peculiar.[19]

Emerson, who had been writing to her for almost four years urging her to come home, had a dramatic change of heart. This was communicated obliquely by the Springs in one of the last letters she received before leaving Italy in May 1850:

[If] you return you will lose the power to write as well for you would not be so happy and your friend (with whom with much pleasure we now learn from Hicks is your old friend Giovanni) would not and could not be so happy here as in his own beautiful Italy — what could repay him, and what could with you take the place of such [illegible] as the Brownings and others you mention? . . . It is because we love you we say 'stay'.[20]

The tragically prophetic and elegiac quality that Fuller's friends, and most of her modern biographers, found in her writing leading up to the family's embarkation on the sailing schooner

45

USS *Elizabeth* at Leghorn in May 1850, continued almost unrelieved throughout the voyage. The ship's master, Captain Hasty, died from smallpox off Gibraltar, the ship was quarantined and he was buried at sea. Angelino then caught the disease but was remarkably nursed back to health.

Finally, after a voyage of over five weeks, with the ship in the hands of an inexperienced mate who misjudged his approach to New York along the southern shore of Long Island, early on 19 July the *Elizabeth* hit a sand bar off Fire Island. Over the next twelve hours, it broke up, a process accelerated by the breaking through the hold by the main cargo of Carrara marble. Contemporary accounts, at least some of which were undoubtedly gilded by hindsight as the fate of the Ossolis' party became clear, are painful to read. Wreckers gathered on the shore, less than a hundred yards away and some sailors (including the mate) escaped. Fuller resolutely refused to be separated from her family and was eventually swept into the sea. Her last words, reported by the cook, were apparently 'I see nothing but death before me, — I shall never reach the shore'.[21]

In spite of a search by Thoreau and others, only Angelino's body was recovered, along with one of the family's chests containing papers and mementoes but not all-important manuscripts. Angelino was finally reburied under a large marble memorial to all three erected by the Fuller family in Mount Auburn cemetery in Massachusetts.

Fuller's actions in the last hours of her life, in so far as they can be reconstructed, have been superimposed on her clearly articulated misgivings about her return to the United States to create a genre of writing about her death which attempts to make of it the final act of a Greek tragedy. This process began early, with Elizabeth Barrett Browning's private eulogy in a letter to a friend, written in 1852:

The work she was preparing in Italy would probably have been more equal to her faculty than anything previously produced by her pen (her other writings being curiously inferior to the impressions her conversation gave you); indeed, she told me it was the only production to which she had given time and labour. But, if rescued, the manuscript would be nothing but the same material. I believe nothing was finished; nor, if finished, could the work have been otherwise than deeply coloured by those blood colours of Socialistic views, which would have drawn the wolves on her, with a still more howling emnity, both in England and America. Therefore it was better for her to go. Only God and a few friends can be expected to distinguish between the pure personality of a woman and her professional opinions.[22]

As for her American friends, and the immediate creators of the 'Margaret Myth', there is no escaping the unhappy conclusion that her death was something of a relief.

During the course of the last century psychological approaches to history and criticism have reinforced rather than relieved this tendency. In 1922 it was important to Katherine Anthony's thesis that the evidence confirmed 'that Margaret had exerted almost no effort from the beginning to end to save herself and her family', in effect 'she submitted to be drowned'.[23] It is my contention that the evidence is just not strong enough to sustain incontrovertibly this analysis of a final and irrevocable choice by Fuller. It is striking, none the less, how irresistible the argument from fate has proved. Not even Chevigny, probably the most effective modern critic of the 'Margaret Myth' (as well as the most self-concious and self-critical), can resist the temptation:

With the loss of that book, fifty yards from the American shore, with the ending of this story in July, 1850, history itself becomes allegorical: it insists the ship must split. Fuller must drown, the book sink beyond recall. A centrifugal force cannot be harnessed to a circle: her ideological trajectory could not return her to her source. Fuller could not come home with all she inevitably would express. The sense of the ending is self-contradictory; it is of the impossibility of reconciliation, a return refused as if by the very nature of things.[24]

# Notes

1. *At Home and Abroad*, p. 225.
2. Ibid, p. 343.
3. Ibid, p. 361.
4. Blanchard, p. 277.
5. *At Home and Abroad*, pp. 251–2.
6. *Memoirs*, III, pp. 154, 152, 149.
7. See Bell Gale Chevigny, 'To the Edges of Ideology: Margaret Fuller's Centrifugal Evolution', *American Quarterly*, 38:2, 1986 (hereafter Chevigny 1986), pp. 173–201; *At Home and Abroad*, pp. 326–7.
8. *At Home and Abroad*, pp. 325–6.
9. Chevigny 1976a, p. 490; *At Home and Abroad*, p. 415.
10. Welter, *Dimity Convictions*, pp. 145–98, quotation p. 193.
11. See Bell Gale Chevigny, 'The Long Arm of Censorship: Myth-making in Margaret Fuller's Time and Our Own', *Signs* 2:2, Winter 1976 (hereafter Chevigny 1976b), pp. 450–60; *Memoirs*, III, p. 145.
12. Stern, pp. 430–1; Deiss, pp. 291–2.
13. *At Home and Abroad*, p. 380.
14. Ibid, pp. 435–6.
15. *Memoirs*, III, p. 216.
16. Ibid, pp. 265–6.
17. Ibid, p. 226.
18. Deiss, p. 282.
19. *Memoirs*, III, p. 282.
20. Chevigny 1976a, p. 400.
21. *At Home and Abroad*, p. 446.
22. Chevigny 1976a, p. 414.
23. Anthony, pp. 205–8.
24. Chevigny 1986, p. 193.

# Part II   The Work

*The Marchese Giovanni Angelo Ossoli*

# 5 Romanticism

Margaret Fuller made a central but rarely acknowledged contribution to the definition of American romanticism. She achieved this in the following ways, in ascending order of importance. First, and especially in the period up to 1845, she produced creative and original work incorporating romantic ideas of self-discovery and of redemption through individual striving. She also employed characteristic romantic modes of expression like symbolism and mysticism. Secondly, she acted as a tutor and facilitator. Here her role was decisive in terms of Goethe and contemporary German literature, but she was also important as a translator and exegete of other European literature. Thirdly, and here her influence has been most lasting, she created the role of national literary critic, initially and tentatively as editor of *The Dial* and then with growing confidence and scope for the *New York Tribune* from New York and Europe.

Fuller was thus an important, but relatively submerged, figure in the movement of American letters identified, rather archly, by F.O. Matthiessen in 1941 as *The American Renaissance*. She deserves to stand beside not only her transcendentalist colleagues (Emerson and Thoreau) but also the leading literary artists of the mid-century: Poe, Hawthorne, Melville and Whitman. All shared some important aspects of the American romantic programme, and a common debt to some of the key ideas of transcendentalism. These ranged from the centrality of individual insight in fixing man's place in society, through the development of symbolic and metaphorical 'correspondences' to, perhaps most importantly, a collective contribution to the mythic framework of American democracy.[1]

Fuller's achievement has been at best confused and at worst suppressed for a number of reasons. Her contemporaries with a few shining exceptions took an aloof and somewhat patronising attitude to much of her original work. After her death they then encouraged critical attention to concentrate on aspects of her personality rather than her writing. Her output was admittedly variable. She struggled with poetry as a form, which she felt she had to master in order fully to express her feelings yet which continually frustrated her. Indeed the resolution of her search for a form was not fully achieved except in her letters (which, like a good transcendentalist, she regarded as preliminary exercises) and finally in her mature journalism.[2] Defining this struggle against the moral and intellectual concerns of her contemporaries is a vital prerequisite for a full evaluation of her literary success.

The New England generation in which Fuller grew up was undergoing an intellectual upheaval, usually cast in theological terms. The Puritan Theocracy had, of course, come to an end, and the battle that finally broke it — between orthodox Calvinists and liberal Unitarians — had resulted in two opposing centres of power and influence: the Presbyterian Congregationalists at Princeton and the theological seminaries, and the Unitarians, led triumphantly in Boston from Harvard University and its Divinity School. At the time of Emerson's formal education a few years before Fuller's involvement with the 'class of '29', the chief spokesmen of the two wings were Moses Stuart, professor at Andover Theological Seminary from 1810–45, and Andrews Norton, who resigned from the Dexter Professorship of Sacred Literature in the Harvard Divinity School in 1830 in order to devote himself to the defence of liberal Christianity put forward in his *Evidences of the Genuineness of the Gospels* (1837, 1844).

The liberal's main weapon against the Calvinists had been the use of Enlightenment thought, with its emphasis on the powers of human reason as established by Locke and demonstrated by Newton, to counter the hardline insistence on human depravity and utter reliance for salvation on the infusion of divine grace. One of the clearest and most helpful ways to assess transcendentalism is against this theological spectrum; as a version of the liberal objection to Calvinism that developed so far as to destroy the epistemological underpinnings of Unitarianism. Emerson and his followers took cues from the more advanced liberal thinkers, particularly William Ellery Channing (the founder in 1820 of the Berry Street conference — an important forum for Unitarian ministers in Boston), to develop the self-reliance of the individual soul beyond the boundaries that formal Enlightenment reasoning would wish to set for it. Channing had at one stage proclaimed an 'essential sameness' between man and God. Against this the liberal and orthodox wings had common cause. Their version of the 'moral sense' was limited to the 'common sense' theory of the Scottish realists — Thomas Reid, Dugald Stewart, and pre-eminently Sir William Hamilton — which expanded the empiricist psychology of Locke to include sentiments, emotion and conscience in the description of how we interpret the world. Essentially this theory implied that intuitions of the conscience would coincide in all right-thinking men. The individualism of Emerson's personal 'angle of vision' thus opened the gate to solipsistic heresy.

At Harvard the leadership of the defensive case was assumed by Francis Bowen, whose career spanned the two main campaigns fought by the Unitarian hierarchy: the skirmish with the transcendentalists, which they won; and the war with Darwinian evolution, which they lost. Bowen's interests were impressively wide. He edited the *North American Review* from 1843–54. He published textbook versions of Hamilton and Stewart, and the first American translation of De Tocqueville's *Democracy in America*. He wrote on economics and politics as well as philosophy. In 1837 his hostile review of Emerson's *Nature* closed the *Christian Examiner*, the organ of New England Liberal theology, to the transcendentalists for good.

None the less, by themselves the internal debates of Unitarianism were not sufficient stimulus for the transcendentalist revolt. This also relied crucially on the absorption of two important currents of European thought into the intellectual milieu. In broad terms these can be labelled German idealism and British romanticism. The assimilation was frequently indirect, and later caused much heart-searching as American intellectual leaders simultaneously tried to establish their independence from European tradition, but just as American puritanism had been unable to resist the European Enlightenment, American romanticism also began with an important reservoir of second-hand ideas. The Unitarians had, in effect, accepted a Trojan Horse into their midst. In 1806 Joseph Stevens Buckminster, the minister of the Brattle Street church (Boston's foremost Unitarian congregation), went on a trip to Europe and brought back the 3,000 volumes that formed the nucleus of the Library of the Boston Atheneum. Equally subversive were the early translations and reviews — for example of Cousin, Coleridge and Carlyle — which appeared in the *Christian Examiner*.

In this way several interesting figures, who cannot strictly be called transcendentalists, made vital contributions to the cause. Among them were the historian George Bancroft, who had taken his Ph.D. from the university of Göttingen in 1820, and Fuller's close friend Frederic Henry Hedge, a minister in West Cambridge and later a long-serving Harvard teacher, whose *Prose Writers of Germany* (1848) was the first American anthology of its kind. Hedge also collaborated with several transcendentalists, chiefly George Ripley, on an influential series called *Specimens of Standard Foreign Literature* (in which Fuller's first book appeared). From this array of new material, two publications, in particular, stand out as being helpful to the transcendentalists: the edition of Coleridge's *Aids to Reflection* brought out in 1829 by James Marsh, a staunchly orthodox Calvinist who later taught the young John Dewey at the University of Vermont, and a translation, published in 1832, of Victor Cousin's *Introduction to the History of Philosophy*. The latter provided a dramatically foreshortened and simplified account of the origins and achievement of the idealism of Kant, Schelling and Hegel, none of whom were read seriously in the original (except possibly by Hedge) until later in the century. Such works were, however, sufficient to develop the scene described by Perry Miller: 'About 1825–35 students at Harvard College were in actuality receiving two distinct and disparate educations, one in the classroom, administered by Professors Norton and Bowen, and one in the dormitory, where they were pouring over European importations'.[3]

Among the lessons learnt indirectly from these 'importations' and directly from men like Bancroft, Hedge, and, after his 1832 trip, Emerson himself, was the romantic concept of 'Reason' as a higher intuitive faculty than the empirical understanding. This came chiefly from Coleridge (the transcendentalists were uneasy about Wordsworth and took longer to admire him as either a poet or a thinker). Meanwhile, the German connection gave them both the idealist confidence in the individual's capacity to know and act according to his conscience and, highly significantly, gave them access to the 'higher' or 'historical' criticism of the Bible. It was the appreciation of German biblical critics like Bruno Bauer, David Friedrich Strauss, and, notably, N.M.L. De Wette (whom Parker translated) that led to the great works of transcendentalist theology: William Henry Furness' *Remarks on the Four Gospels*

(1836); the review by Ripley of James Martineau's *Rationale of Religious Enquiry* (also 1836), which provoked Norton into publishing an angry rebuttal in the Boston *Daily Advertiser*; and Theodore Parker's sermon on 'The Transient and Permanent in Christianity' (1841). All of these works focused on the historical rather than the divine personality of Jesus, the irrationality of 'miracles', 'special providences' and other supernatural 'signs' of God's grace, and the duty of the individual soul to devise its own salvation. Against them, to his own great anguish, Norton was eventually forced to join hands with the Presbyterians and republish articles from the conservative *Princeton Review* on Unitarian presses.

In this sense the seed-bed of transcendentalism was religious controversy. Fuller was briefly but significantly a transcendentalist without fully probing the intricacies of her mentors' doctrinal opposition to the Establishment. What she did take from transcendentalism, in addition to its extreme individualism and its demonstration of the liberating possibilities opened up by European literature, was a generalised religious sensibility. In this she reflects, ironically more closely than Emerson himself — if the accuracy of his programme as set out above (Chapter 2) is conceded — the manner in which transcendentalism as a movement has entered the stream of general cultural history.

Into the charged atmosphere of moral debate in Boston and Concord Fuller brought initially little more than the fruits of her domestic and institutional education and a powerful self-image as a personality and an intellect to be reckoned with. Under the guidance of Timothy Fuller and the Prescotts the former had been imaginatively expanded from its classical base to bring her into contact with modern European languages and literature. The latter was an almost inevitable offshoot. In her late teens and early twenties Fuller developed a series of role models derived directly from her reading. These included Aspasia (consort of Pericles in fifth-century Athens), the canoness Karoline Günderode (the correspondent of Goethe's young friend Bettina Brentano), and most prominently Corinne (the heroine of Madame de Staël's novel). When these enthusiasms are combined with her later dramatic exploits, the temptation to overemphasise the drama of Fuller's life as opposed to her art, to which her contemporaries and subsequent generations succumbed, is all the more explicable. Perry Miller's verdict is typical.

> ... in Margaret Fuller, daughter as she was of Puritan New England, we have virtually the only candidate — and in her case an authentic one — for the role of a native champion of the Romantic heroine in the grandiose (and so, for an American, dangerously close to the ludicrous) operatic manner. Only she could prove an equal combatant in the wide arena of feminine intellectuality that up to that time had been pre-empted by Madame de Staël and George Sand. And it seemed further that she possessed the only mind among her contemporaries that could have conversed on a plane of equality (though she brashly self-assumed this) with Rousseau and Goethe.[4]

Such portraits may be colorful, but objectively they can be shown to be unfair. Fuller did not just feed off the work of her male contemporaries for the purposes of self-presentation. In some specific areas she was more influential upon them than vice versa. Her early exercises in interpreting and re-evaluating Goethe are the clearest example, and all the more remarkable given her relative youth and inexperience at the time.

Fuller began to learn German, with Hedge, at the age of sixteen. By 1832 she was already into a mature dialogue with James Freeman Clarke about German literature and ideas, and when the family moved to Groton in 1833 had begun to formulate a 'project' — the life of Goethe. This was never completed (there are some suggestions that in their final form the notes for it were also lost with the *Elizabeth*), but several important publications sprang from it between 1839 and 1840.[5]

The transcendentalists, as indicated above, took much of their literary inspiration from British writers and their key philosophical concepts from the Germans. German literature, especially the work of Goethe, had the reputation of encouraging unbridled sensuality and hence immorality. Fuller simply and bravely ignored these implicit judgements and followed her German interests not towards Kant (indeed she found herself in the position of having to write to Clarke for instant tutorials on the 'history of philosophical opinion in Germany') but towards the imaginative literature.[6] The initial outcomes were translations of Goethe's drama about the Renaissance poet *Torquato Tasso*, which circulated unpublished during her lifetime and convinced Emerson of Fuller's seriousness as a scholar; of the *Conversations* between Goethe and his secretary Johann Eckermann (published in 1839 by George Ripley — her first book); and of parts of the correspondence, which had moved her deeply, between Bettina Brentano and Karoline Günderode before the latter's suicide (a small part of this was published by Elizabeth Peabody in 1842 as *Günderode*, while Fuller's young friend Maria Wesselhoeft, who had lived next door to her in Cambridge, later completed the extended project which was published in 1861).[7] Russell Durning has established both the quality of these translations and the use made of them by scholars of German from the mid-century onwards. More immediate was the impact of Fuller's advocacy of Goethe, as set out in her preface to the *Conversations* and two lengthy essays in *The Dial*.

The contemporary American estimate of Goethe was almost uniformly negative. His work was seen as encouraging immorality and self-centredness of a different and more corrosive kind to that favoured by the transcendentalists and unitarians. In characteristic fashion these failures were also identified in what little was known of his life. Fuller's view of Goethe was not uncritical and she puzzled to the end of her life about his character. For example, she confided in her journal her disappointment at his abandonment of his lover Lili Schoemann before he, in her view, exiled himself in Weimar.

I have thought much whether Goethe did well in giving up Lili. That was the crisis in his existence. From that era dates his being as a 'Weltweise'; the heroic element vanished irrecoverably from his character; he became an Epicurean and a Realist; plucking flowers and hammering stones instead of looking at the stars. How could he look through the blinds, and see her sitting alone in her beauty, yet give her up for so slight reasons? He was right as a genius, but wrong as a character.[8]

Disappointed and puzzled though she might have been by such aspects of her hero, Fuller was equally certain of Goethe's innocence of the simplistic and ignorant charges generally laid against him. In her preface to the *Conversations* she laid these out dramatically.

57

The objections, so far as I know them, may be resolved into these classes —

He is not a Christian;

He is not an idealist;

He is not a democrat;

He is not Schiller.

Beyond showing the extent to which these prejudices rested on a partial and unsympathetic reading of Goethe, Fuller did not at this early stage fully substantiate her counter-case, and relied on future progress in critical judgements. 'The greatness of Goethe his nation has felt for more than half a century; the world is beginning to feel it, but time may not yet have ripened his critic; especially as the grand historical standpoint is the only one from which a comprehensive view could be taken of him.'

Within two years Fuller was, however, prepared to meet her own challenge. In the longer of her two *Dial* essays, published in July 1841, she presents a systematic account of the sequence of Goethe's major works, finding in each a progressive description of universal human emotions. In her view the life and the work represented its own kind of moral striving: 'he was neither Epicurean nor sensualist, if we consider his life as a whole'. *Faust*, for example, 'contains the great idea of his life, as indeed there is but one great poetic idea possible to man — the progress of a soul through the various forms of existence'. This process of rehabilitation included even the notorious *Elective Affinities*, which in its account of barely suppressed adulterous attractions under a single roof, most served to shock Goethe's New England readers.[9]

Although many of Fuller's critical comments were inextricably wound up with her own personal dilemmas (she wrote of Goethe, 'I too have been disturbed by his aversion to pain and isolation of the heart'), the case made for her pivotal position by scholars of the nineteenth-century American reception of German culture is unassailable. Henry Pochmann puts the point about this debt owed to Fuller by her philosophical mentors bluntly: 'More than any other single influence, her activity as reviewer, translator and conversationalist was the agency that brought German literature into the orbit of the Transcendentalist's interests'.[10]

By the early 1840s the transcendentalists' inner council had unwittingly placed Fuller in a position of even greater influence.

When they made her editor of *The Dial* it is highly unlikely that they anticipated the determined and independent way she was to use her role. As Bernard Rosenthal concludes: 'From 1840 to 1842 *The Dial* was more the journal of Margaret Fuller than it was the journal of the transcendentalists'.[11]

Fuller's editorial teeth were felt in several ways. First she insisted on her own standards of clarity in writing, rejecting submissions from Channing, Alcott and Thoreau and even daring to correct the expression of Emerson. Secondly, she took a firm line over the appropriateness of the content of submissions. As a consequence the numbers under her control appear in a more uncomplicated romantic mould than Emerson and others of his circle would have preferred. There is a heavy emphasis on literature, art and music (especially her German favourites) while the social criticism is restricted almost entirely to the religious commentary of Theodore Parker. Emerson objected in the following terms: 'I would not have it too purely literary. I wish we might make a journal so broad and great in the survey that it should lead the opinion of this generation on every great interest, and read the law on property, government, education, as well as on art, letters, and religion'.[12]

One effect of these editorial undertakings was that Fuller had to work at a frenzied pace to meet the waves of deadlines that rushed up on her. She was almost as busy writing to solicit and remind contributors of their obligations as she was in correcting and returning their work. When she could not find enough to meet her own stern tests she simply raided her own notebooks and journal. For the modern reader the join shows, particularly in the early numbers, where her own poetry, reviews and 'dialogues' top up the volumes to their statutory length. In October 1843 she wrote more than half of the entire issue. More constructively, however, she was able to use the pages of *The Dial* as an important testing ground for her own writing. The work she produced is surprisingly varied.

Fuller's imaginative contributions to *The Dial* show her at the peak of her experimentation with romantic forms and ideas. In the period Emerson describes her as going through a phase of 'ecstatic solitude' (perhaps not unconnected with her romantic failures with both Ward and himself), which achieved literary form in her obsession with mythology, daemonology, the symbolic values of flowers and stones, and emblems like the sistrum. An example is the fantasy 'Leila' which appeared in April 1841, including what seems now to be an idealised self-portrait.

> Most men, as they gazed on Leila were pained; they left her at last baffled and well-nigh angry. For most men are bound in sense, time and thought. They shrink from the overflow of the infinite; they cannot a moment abide in the coldness of abstractions; the weight of an idea is too much for their lives . . . And men called Leila mad, because they felt she made them so.[13]

The style and tone of these 'creative' items, heavily symbolic and self-absorbed, sits somewhat uneasily alongside Fuller's more extensive contribution of critical essays and reviews to all four volumes of the journal. These complete a neat circle; Volume I opens with 'A Short Essay on Critics' and Volume IV (July 1843) with 'The Great Lawsuit' (Fuller also had the last word, as the last number, in April 1844, closes with one of her dialogues). In the critical essays Fuller set some clear standards, and tried to live up to them. Her ideal was of the 'comprehensive' critic, who could rise above both the 'subjective' class (those content with 'mere records of impression') and the 'apprehensive' (who can 'go out of themselves and enter fully into a foreign existence'). Comprehensive critics ('who must also be apprehensive') know how to put an author's 'aim in its place, and how to estimate its relations'. They are, in short, 'men with the practical temperament to apprehend, with the philosophical tendency to investigate'.[14]

Armed with these intentions Fuller not only used *The Dial* to rehabilitate and explain Goethe and his contemporaries, but also to work towards the map of contemporary American Literature and its potential which she was to complete in the *New York Tribune* and *Papers on Literature and Art*. In *The Dial* reviews Hawthorne comes in for particular praise, but the overall picture is not optimistic. As Fuller remarks in the course of a witty résumé of 'Entertainments of the Past Winter': 'Life is living, and art, European art lives in the opera and ballet. For us we have nothing of our own, for the same reason that in literature, a few pale buds is all that we yet can boast of native growth, because we have no national character of sufficient fulness and simplicity to demand it'. In contrast to the European artistic cornucopia, New England's selected form is 'the Lecture'.[15]

Fuller was the most consistent and prolific contributor to *The Dial* evn after she was forced to give up the editorship in the summer of 1843. Her work in it did not, however, exhaust her role in the definition of American romanticism. There is also the largely second-hand account of her extension of many of her key themes in the 'Conversations', and more concretely the product of her post-editorial western vacation, *Summer on the Lakes*.

As noted above, the latter is on one level an example of another familiar transcendentalist literary form, that of 'writing-through' moral and metaphysical problems from the standpoint of subjective experience. Many of its more curious episodes — the 'Mariana fable'; the long story of a traveller encountered on the Lakes called 'P', who spent a life sentence of a marriage atoning for his 'hour of passion'; the contest of 'Self-Poise' and 'True Hope'; and a lengthy extract from Justinus Kerner's account of a famous contemporary clairvoyant *The Seeress of Prevorst* (1831) — link obviously with Fuller's personal dilemmas and enthusiasms. Running throughout, however, is a powerful thread of exhortatory criticism. The energy of life on the frontier is praised almost to the same extent as the utilitarian values it embodies are deplored (after standing in awe at the majesty of the Niagara Falls, where 'there is no escape from the weight of a perpetual creation', Fuller describes the fellow-traveller who claims the scene by spitting into it). Similarly the irreversible wrongs done to native Americans ('I can scarely see how they can forbear to shoot the white man where he stands') are balanced by the possibilities of foreign immigration and racial amalgamation.[16]

By the time she had embarked on her new career in New York the more expressive phase of Fuller's romanticism was over. Indeed, in the critical record not much of her imaginative work (including a single attempt at fiction) has survived as worthy of note.[17] Her experience in New York and Europe, and the particular nature of Horace Greeley's assignments, enabled her to more than make up for this recession in her reputation as a creative writer with her development as a critic. As a self-consciously 'national' critic her chief method was comparative. She simultaneously announced and explained the literature of Germany, France, Italy and Spain; and attempted to estimate the success of her fellow-Americans in meeting the challenge. The latter enterprise included some celebrated hits and misses. I have already dealt with her recognition of Hawthorne and neglect of Poe — her closest critical rival — as well as the growing confidence with which she was able to put Emerson in his place. Not even her kindest critics have been able to explain or justify her rehabilitation of Charles Brockden Brown, author of the Gothic mysteries *Wieland; or the Transformation* (1798) and *Ormond; or the Secret Witness* (1799) except perhaps because of his reputation as an early feminist.

Fuller's growing sense of national destiny was as fully romantic as that of any of the contemporary Europeans she so admired. It was also coupled with the democratic ideals later to be expressed so forcibly by American romantics like Whitman and Melville. Her peroration in 'American Literature' significantly antedates the Civil War and the post-war redefinitions of national character.

What suits Great Britain, with her insular position and consequent need to concentrate and intensify her life, her limited monarchy, and spirit of trade, does not suit a mixed race, continually enriched with new blood from other stocks the most unlike that of our first descent, with ample field and verge enough to range in and leave every impulse free, and abundant opportunity to developed [sic] a genius, wide and full as our rivers, flowery, luxuriant and impassioned as our vast prairies, rooted in strength as the rocks on which the Puritan fathers landed. . .
That day will not rise till the fusion of races among us is more complete. It will not rise till this nation shall attain sufficient moral and intellectual dignity to prize moral and intellectual, no less highly than political, freedom, not till, the physical resources of the country being explored, all its regions studded with towns, broken by the plow, netted together by railways and telegraph lines, talent shall be left at leisure to turn its energies upon the higher department of man's existence.[19]

Fuller's romanticism was not unusual in carrying such a large burden of nationalistic fervour. This explains simply much of her affinity with Mazzini. It also helps to explain her transformation into a socialist. Her final estimate of American destiny was in fact achieved in political terms, once she had distanced herself from the country, and in ways which would have deeply shocked her transcendentalist collaborators. However, before examining how Fuller's romanticism ended in socialism it is necessary to take a detour, to estimate the relationship of both to her feminism: the aspect of her work for which she has been most consistently feted in the century-and-a-third since her death.

# Notes

1. F.O. Matthiessen, *American Renaissance: Art and Expression in the Age of Emerson and Whitman*, New York and Oxford: Oxford U. Press, 1974 (repr. of 1941 edn); see also Robert D. Richardson, *Myth and Literature in the American Renaissance*, Bloomington: Indiana U. Press, 1978.
2. See Margaret V. Allen, 'This Impassioned Yankee: Margaret Fuller's Writing Revisited', *Southwest Review*, 58, 1972, pp. 162–71.
3. Perry Miller (ed.), *The Transcendentalists: An Anthology*, Cambridge, Mass.: Harvard U. Press, 1971 (repr. of 1950 edn), p. 12.
4. Miller (ed.), *Margaret Fuller*, pp. xii–xiii.
5. See Russell E. Durning, *Margaret Fuller, Citizen of the World: An Intermediary between European and American Literature*, Heidelberg: Carl Winter Universitätsverlag, 1969, pp. 83–129 (hereafter Durning).
6. *Letters*, II, p. 244; for Clarke's reply see *The Letters of James Freeman Clarke to Margaret Fuller*, ed. John Wesley Thomas, Hamburg: Cram, de Gruyte & Co., 1957, pp. 113–16.
7. Durning, pp. 109–15; for publication details see Myerson (ed.), *Critical Essays*, p. ix.
8. *Life Without and Life within*, p. 350.
9. Chevigny 1976a, pp. 176 and 181: *Life Without and Life Within*, pp. 20–51.
10. Henry A. Pochmann, extract from *German Culture in America* (1957), in Myerson (ed.), *Critical Essays*, p. 228.
11. Bernard Rosenthal, '*The Dial*, Transcendentalism, and Margaret Fuller', *English Language Notes*, 8, 1970, pp. 28–36.
12. See George Willis Cooke, *An Historical and Biographical Introduction to Accompany the Dial*, 2 vols., New York: Russell & Russell, 1961 (repr. of 1902 edn), I, pp. 76–7.
13. *Memoirs*, II, p. 106; *The Dial*, 4 vols., New York: Russell & Russell, 1961 (repr.), I.3, April 1841, pp. 462–7.
14. *The Dial*, I.1, July 1840, pp. 5–11.

15. *The Dial*, III.1, July 1842, pp. 46–72.
16. *Summer on the Lakes*, pp. 61–2, 68–9 and 96–7.
17. See Alexander E. Jones, 'Margaret Fuller's Attempt to Write Fiction', *Boston Public Library Quarterly*, 6, 1954, pp. 67–73.
18. Durning, pp. 31–3.
19. *Papers on Literature and Art*, pp. 122–4; on Melville and Whitman see Anne Norton, *Alternative Americas: A Reading of Antebellum Political Culture*, Chicago and London: U. Chicago Press, 1986, pp. 278–92 and 315–29.

# 6 Feminism

The concept of feminism is multi-layered. At its root it depends upon taking gender seriously as a category of social analysis. At its apex it provides prescriptions for political action, by and on behalf of women. Fuller's career and writing exhibit the former, from an early stage up to her last writings. What is more, she soon identified features of the social and cultural condition of American and western European women in the mid-nineteenth century that went beyond conventional wisdom about the 'separate spheres' of male and female.

Fuller's attention to the political dimension of her feminist convictions was less consistent. Building on ideas she developed while working in her first position of authority among her peers, as editor of *The Dial*, she published America's first widely-read feminist tract. Subsequently *Woman in the Nineteenth Century* has proved more important for its aura than for its content. Fuller's political and cultural preoccupations in the last five years of her life included women in wider, and from the feminist point of view, less focused plans for human liberation.

As a school-teacher, and not least as a consequence of her own peculiar education, Fuller developed a special sympathy for, and a strikingly analytical approach towards her female pupils. A consistent theme was her recognition of the superficiality which even the most enlightened and broad curriculum encouraged on the part of girls. In addition to her own records and thoughts (including the farewell to Greene Street quoted on page 10 above) we have the testimony of one of her pupils, Anna Gale, who kept a journal. This gives examples of Fuller's wit, humanity, and occasional firmness and lack of flexibility. But it speaks most strongly about the ways in which the 28-year-old teacher urged her charges (most of whom were eighteen or nineteen) to reflect systematically on what they were reading. Her text was Francis Wayland's *Elements of Moral Science* (1834), more usually employed as a course for college students. This, for example, is how Gale describes her exposition of 'the great doctrine of atonement':

Miss Fuller stated to us the two different views which were taken of it, saying that she did not wish to influence us in favour or against either, or hurt anyone's feelings. Some thought it meant reconciliation; that Jesus by his death showed us how we might be reconciled with God; that he thus testified his divine mission, by being ready to seal it with his blood. Others suppose that Jesus was offered as a sacrifice for an atonement of the sins of the world; that he bore the weight of the sins of all who lived before, and all who would live after him. And they think that none, however good their lives may appear, can enjoy happiness hereafter unless they have this belief, but this faith cannot exist without works.

There is ample evidence of the kind of magnetic spell which Fuller cast over many of her pupils. Gale (who seems to have been less susceptible than some) includes a letter from her friend Mary Allen: 'Miss Fuller is as dear as ever — says she would rather have you back than to have three new scholars — I think she is *less satirical* than last term, & I love her more than words can tell'.[1] This, of course, was appreciated and suspected by Fuller in almost equal measure. It was also a feature of her audience for her similar exercises in adult education.

Suspicious perhaps of the content of the Boston 'Conversations', some feminists have striven to make them more significant for the fact of their organisation (and, until 1841, their female exclusivity). Dale Spender sees them as an early example of women's studies, as they attempted to set up 'an educational programme for women, *outside* the institutions controlled by men'.[2] The programme and delivery of the sessions, like the information we have about her school-teaching, indeed show Fuller attempting to initiate women into what she understood to be a male-dominated world of reflection about the romantic verities. The only hint of a specific angling of the material is the description of one series as devoted to 'the proper influence of women on family, school, church, society and literature', which at this stage is unlikely to have been as radical as it might sound. With hindsight, the apparent avoidance of political topics has led to an interpretation of her life in Boston as at best quiescent. In the loaded words of Harriet Martineau, at its worst it was a 'little short of destructive'.[3]

Privately, however, Fuller's critique of the sexual balance of power was developing apace. Her papers include an undated fragment, the tone and style of which suggest strongly that it was written in the early 1840s: '*Woman — Man —* Woman is the flower, man the bee. She sighs out melodious fragrance, and invites the winged laborer. He drains her up, and carries off the honey. She dies on the stalk; he returns to the hive, well fed, and praised as an active member of the community'.[4] More concretely, *Summer on the Lakes* contains a firm critique of two aspects of the contemporary relationship between the sexes.

Some of her most acute observations of life in the West concern the difficulties experienced by settler women, as a consequence of a traditional view of marriage and the lack of appropriate preparation for life on the frontier.

It has generally been the choice of the men, and the women follow, as women will, doing their best for affection's sake, but too often in heart-sickness and weariness. Beside, it frequently not being a choice or conviction of their own minds that it is best to be here, their part is the hardest, and they are least fitted for it. . . .

The women can rarely find any aid in domestic labor. All its various and careful tasks must often be performed, sick or well, by the mother and daughters, to whom a city education has imparted neither the strength nor skill now demanded.

The wives of the poorer settlers, having more hard work to do than before, very frequently become slatterns; but the ladies, accustomed to a refined neatness, feel that they can degrade themselves by its absence, and struggle under every disadvantage to keep up the necessary nature of small arrangements.

Deploring the fact that they have 'not learnt to ride, to drive, to row alone', and that their education has generally been to prepare them to be 'ornaments of society', Fuller's chief and characteristic concern is for the daughters of this first generation of frontier wives:

. . . they have a great deal to work with in the habits of thought acquired by their mothers from their own early life. Everywhere the fatal spirit of imitation, of reference to European standards, penetrates, and threatens to blight whatever of original growth might adorn the soil . . . If the little girls grow up strong, resolute, able to exert their faculties, their mothers mourn over their want of fashionable delicacy . . . their grand ambition for their children is to send them to school in some Eastern city, the measure most likely to make them useless and happy at home.

For the settler women there is optimism that their destiny might be in their own hands.

To a girl really skilled to make home beautiful and comfortable, with bodily strength to enjoy plenty of exercise, the woods, the streams, a few studies, music, and the sincere and familiar intercourse, far more easily to be met here than elsewhere, would afford happiness enough. Her eyes would not grow dim, nor her cheeks sunken, in the absence of parties, morning visits and milliners' shops.

For the Indian women Fuller encountered the prospects were bleaker, as in her eyes they would bear the brunt of the enforced degradation of the race to compound their unequal treatment within the tribe.

Notwithstanding the homage paid to women, and the consequence allowed them in some cases, it is impossible to look upon the Indian women without feeling that they *do* occupy a lower place than women among the natives of European civilization . . . More weariness than anguish, no doubt, fall to the lot of most of these women. They inherit submission, and the minds of the generality accommodate themselves more or less to any posture. Perhaps they suffer less than their white sisters, who have more aspiration and refinement, with little power of self-sustenance. But their place is certainly lower, and their share of the human inheritance less.'[5]

Back in Boston, and directing her literary attentions to work on *The Dial*, Fuller, to the mild astonishment of her collaborators, collected many of these thoughts together and produced her longest personal contribution to the journal. 'The Great Lawsuit: Man *versus* Men; Woman *versus* Women', published in July 1843, was one of the items which most impressed Greeley, whose suggestion it was that it be developed into book form. Over a final vacation, mainly designed to gather her strength for New York, Fuller gave way over the title (she preferred the original), added almost fifty pages, rewrote some other passages in generally more forceful language, and produced *Woman in the Nineteenth Century*. She finished in mid-November 1844. By February 1845 Greeley had published it from his paper's offices in Nassau Street. The work thus preceded Fuller's career as a journalist rather than in any way originating from it.

In the Whig theory of feminism Fuller's *Woman in the Nineteenth Century* is a landmark, standing between Mary Wollstonecraft's *Vindication of the Rights of Women* (1792) and the Seneca Falls Convention of 1848, with its 'Declaration of Sentiments' for women. Fuller is credited both with establishing a more modern and American idiom for Wollstonecraft's moral claim for equality as well as providing a 'manual' in the style of John Locke for the Seneca Falls delegates.[6] Estimates of the book's importance to this tradition range from the prosaic — 'Margaret Fuller introduced to America the genre of women's liberation books' (Bernard Rosenthal, her modern editor) — to the universal — 'the intellectual foundation of the feminist movement' (Marie Urbanski, quoted by Dale Spender).[7]

Because of its form *Woman in the Nineteenth Century* almost defies summary. Orestes Brownson, then a member of the transcendentalist circle and broadly sympathetic, described it as having 'neither beginning, middle, nor end, [it] . . . may be read backwards as well as forwards'. This impression has stuck with some of its modern champions; Margaret Allen, for example, refers to the 'air of improvisation' which it carries. For Urbanski, who has paid the closest scholarly attention to this aspect, its loose and episodic construction in fact conceals a systematic adherence to the classic form of a sermon or oration. According to her scheme, an initial exhortation is followed progressively by a clear proposition (that 'woman needs her turn, and that improvement of her lot would aid in the reformation of men, too'), a partition (or analysis) of the subject, a long section of digression (or sermon-like examples), a series of specific applications to contemporary life, and a final peroration. The latter ends in prayer to God and a poem full of biblical allusion.

For the power to whom we bow

Has given its pledge that, if not now,
They of pure and steadfast mind,
By faith exalted, truth refined,
*Shall* hear all music loud and clear,
Whose first notes they ventured here.[8]

What conceals the logic of this structure, according to Urbanski, is Fuller's commitment to a number of features of transcendentalist method (including the rejection of syllogistic
reasoning) as well as the pamphlet's conversational style. Certainly it is easy to see echoes of contemporary reports of the
Boston 'Conversations' series here, with the long sentences, full of
parenthetic asides, accumulation of examples, and frequent
exhortatory interludes. Spender's summary follows Urbanski's
without referring to the detail of the classical form: '*Woman in the
Nineteenth Century* is an attempt to provide a feminist symbolic
framework in which women's existence can be located and made
meaningful: it is a panorama of women and their lives with a
sub-text which argues for their equality'.[9]

From the kaleidoscopic array of arguments and examples put
forward by Fuller, the strongest unifying theme is her account of
the origin and effects of the separation of male and female
spheres. The most radical of her ideas centre on what is to be
done about it:

> Meanwhile, not a few believe and now themselves have
> expressed the opinion that the time is come when Eurydice is to
> call for an Orpheus, rather than Orpheus for Eurydice; that the
> idea of Man, however imperfectly brought out, has been far
> more so that that of Woman; that she, the other half of the
> same thought, the other chamber of the heart of life, needs now
> take her turn in the full pulsation, and that improvement in the
> daughters will best aid in the reformation of the sons of this
> age.[10]

Most important for Fuller, in this recalibration of the oppor-
tunities available to Man and Woman, is the moral basis on
which the reform is to be effected: 'We would have every arbitrary
barrier thrown down. We would have very path laid open to
Woman as freely as to Man'. It is a fallacy to assume that Man
will take care of Woman's interests. 'Can we think that he takes a

sufficiently discerning and religious view of her office and destiny *ever* to do her justice, except when prompted by sentiment?' The resulting 'harmony of the spheres' will not only occur when 'inward and outward freedom for Women as much as for Man shall be acknowledged as a *right*, not yielded as a concession. As the friend of the negro assumes that one man cannot by right hold another in bondage, so should the friend of Woman assume that Man cannot by right lay even well-meant restriction on Woman'.[11] In discussing the separation of generic Man into its two spheres (Energy and Harmony; Power and Beauty; Intellect and Love), Fuller not only recognises how the male has abused his power, but also how this rebounded upon him ('your punishment is its wickedness'):

Man, in the order of time, was developed first; as energy comes before harmony; power before beauty.

Woman was therefore under his care as an elder. He might have been her guardian and leader.

But, as human nature goes not straight forward, but by excessive action and then reaction in an undulated course, he misunderstood and abused his advantages, and became her temporal master instead of her spiritual sire.

On himself came the punishment. He educated Woman more as a servant than a daughter, and found himself a king without a queen.[12]

For all of the range of examples from literature and contemporary life with which Fuller develops these arguments, there are some only thinly disguised autobiographical currents at work. Her first substantial digression tells the story of Miranda and her education by her father ('a man who cherished no sentimental reverence for woman, but a firm belief in the equality of the sexes'). The outcome, in Miranda's words, was that

Religion was early awakened in my soul, — a sense that what the soul is capable to ask it must attain, and that, though I might be aided and instructed by these, I must depend upon myself as the only constant friend. This self-dependence, which was honored in me, is deprecated as a fault in most women. They are taught to learn their rule from without, not to unfold it from within.

71

Miranda concludes her tale: 'Let it not be said, whenever there is energy or creative genius, "She has a masculine mind"'. Similar hints of personal experience run through Fuller's later discussion of successes of female authorship and female education. 'Too much is said of women being better educated, that they may become better companions and mothers *for men*.'[13]

As for effecting change, in addition to calling upon men to surrender some of their power, and the 'arbitrary barriers' it sustains, Fuller has some strong strictures for women if they are to avoid colluding with the exercise of this power. Some of those she most admired (including George Sand) do not meet her more severe tests:

> Those who would reform the world must show that they do not speak in the heat of wild impulse; their lives must be unsustained by passionate error; they must be severe lawgivers to themselves. They must be religious students of the divine purpose with regard to man, if they would not confound the fancies of a day with the requisitions of eternal good.[14]

Later, separating Woman's nature into its own masculine and feminine parts ('Minerva' and the 'Muse'), Fuller is more explicit about what she means:

> It is . . . only in the present crisis that the preference is given to Minerva. The power of continence must establish the legitimacy of freedom, the power of self-poise the perfection of motion. . . . It is therefore that, while any elevation, in the view of union, is to be hailed with joy, we shall not decline celibacy as the great fact of the time. . . Union is possible only to those who are units. To be fit for relations in time, souls, whether of Man or Woman, must be able to do without them in the spirit . . . men do *not* look at both sides, and woman must leave off asking this and being influenced by them, but retire within themselves, and explore the groundwork of life till they find their peculiar secret.[15]

If *Woman in the Nineteenth Century* is to be read as within the genre of contemporary 'advice' or 'how-to' books, as Barbara Welter suggests it should, Fuller was proposing some extremely radical ideas in a context where no state even recognised the legitimacy of female ownership of property (New York was to be the first in 1849). Evocation of female purity, and even the special qualities of female 'mysticism' and 'electrical magnetism' was fair enough. However, the exposure of male double standards, in such spheres as prostitution ('Women are accustomed to be told by men that the reform is to come *from them*), chivalry ('The bribe is not worth the prize'), and reactions to female originality and creativity, proved instantly controversial. But probably most shocking of all was the direct and forthright way in which Fuller linked questions of sex and passion with her quasi-political programme of female liberation: 'But if you ask me what offices they may fill, I reply — any. I do not care what case you put; let them be sea-captains, if you will.'[16]

A cold-eyed modern reading finds *Woman in the Nineteenth Century* unsatisfactory in many ways. Its inflated style and loose, repetitious structure jar, despite Urbanski's explanation of both. Indeed stylistically it reverses some of the progress shown in *Summer on the Lakes*. As a political tract it can be made to appear anodyne: the moral value of abolitionism is conceded (here Fuller had marched much more slowly than several of her transcendentalist sisters), and her concerns about native Americans repeated, but the book is silent, or at least equivocal, on the question of female suffrage. Modern feminists also have difficulty with Fuller's idealisation of marriage: she outlines four levels of which the highest ('the religious, which may be expressed as pilgrimage towards a common shrine') is described in such terms as to be unattainable in contemporary society. More durable have proved her original ideas on the use of role models, on androgyny ('there is no wholly masculine man, no purely feminine woman'), and on self-reliance and what she calls 'self-impulse': 'I have urged on Woman independence of Man, not that I do not think the sexes mutually needed by one another, but because in Woman this fact has led to an excessive devotion, which has cooled love, degraded marriage, and prevented either sex from being what it should be to itself or the other'.[17]

Fuller's journalism, from New York and then from Europe, continued several of the themes of *Woman in the Nineteenth Century*. She placed before her readers the plight of women who were poor, prostitutes or prisoners, as well as her delight in discovery of further examples of women breaking the bounds of what society found acceptable.

An example of the former is her description of the guide who introduced her and her companions to the lodgings of weavers in Lyons.

My sweet little girl turned out to be a wife of six or seven years' standing, with two rather sickly-looking children; she seemed to have the greatest comfort that is possible amid the perplexities of a hard and anxious lot, to judge by the proud and affectionate manner in which she always said '*mon mari*,' and by the courteous gentleness of his manner toward her. . . . This poor, lovely little girl, at an age when the merchant's daughters of Boston and New York are just gaining their first experience of 'society,' knew to a farthing the price of every article of food and clothing that is wanted by such a household. Her thought by day and her dream by night was, whether she should long be able to procure a scanty supply of these, and Nature had gifted her with precisely those qualities, which, unembarrassed by care, would have made her and all she loved really happy; and she was fortunate now, compared with many of her sex in Lyons, — of whom a gentleman who knows the class well said: 'When the work fails, they have no resource except in the sale of their persons. There are but two ways open to them, weaving or prostitution, to gain their bread.'[18]

On the loftier plane, in addition to describing for her readers several of her social conquests, Fuller enjoyed passing on information such as the following.

Passing from Florence, I came to Bologna — learned Bologna; indeed an Italian city, full of expression, of physiognomy, so to speak. A woman should love Bologna, for there has the spark of intellect in woman been cherished with reverent care. Not in former ages only, but in this, Bologna raised a woman who was worthy to the dignities of its University, and in their Certosa they proudly show the monument to Mathilda Tambroni, late Greek Professor there. . . . In their anatomical hall in the bust of a woman, Professor of Anatomy. . . .

In Milan, also, I see in the Ambrosian Library the bust of a female mathematician. These things make one feel that, if the state of woman in Italy is so depressed, yet a good-will toward a better is not wholly wanting.[19]

The descriptive tone of these passages is revealing. During her stay in Europe Fuller's theoretical reflections about society and the conditions of social progress came to be more widely cast than the original ideas in *Woman in the Nineteenth Century* had promised. This provoked some important re-evaluations, not only of individuals like George Sand (with whom, after their meeting, Fuller was clearly even more sympathetic), but also of institutions like marriage. The willing acceptance of the limitations, as well as the satisfactions of her relationship with Ossoli is a poignant reminder of a personal retreat from some of the more extreme statements of 1844, as well as of the fact that, for Fuller, female emancipation was by then no more than a sub-set of a wider republican and socialist vision.

In these circumstances it is hardly surprising that the development, from the mid-1840s onwards, of political feminism in the United States, Great Britain and France, passed Fuller by. The touchstones of this movement — chiefly reform of property legislation and the campaign for the suffrage — were not prime preoccupations for her.[20] Indeed I have been unable to find a single instance of a reflection during the height of her political activism on behalf of the Roman Revolution that her role was circumscribed by her sex or the attitude towards it of her collaborators.

It is easier then to end this section by identifying what Fuller's mature feminism was not rather than what it was. Katherine Anthony suggested that it was the abstraction of her ideas that moved her apart from the mainstream: 'Her philosophical feminism became indigestible for those engaged in the intense and single-minded propagation for the ballot'.[21] I suggest that it was not so much abstraction as breadth of focus that shifted her work from concern with female liberation to social, although class-based liberation. Throughout she remained a feminist and sensitive to the interpersonal and other problems that arose from contemporary social construction of women's roles. Chevigny's limitation of her feminism to a phase of her career and by aspects of her character is not fully persuasive. In making the latter case she writes:

In a sense, it is remarkable that Fuller became a feminist at all. Certainly identification with other women did not come easily to her. In the absence of a movement, criticism of other women was the natural recourse of a woman seeking to break out of the limited world her sisters seemed to accept, and this was accentuated in Fuller's case by her goals of unlimited self-development. To defend herself from discouragement, Fuller cultivated in private her sense of exceptionality and prescribed herself publicly as a woman of singular destiny. Her feminism never eradicated these habits.[22]

By the end of her life these characteristics, if they had indeed previously resulted in the effects Chevigny suggests (which seem to belie at least some of her reputation as a *confidante*), were considerably muted. The 'confessions' about her personal dilemmas to female friends and family, coded as they were, reveal a sense of reciprocal reliance that comes close to modern feminist concepts of mutual support. By then, of course, Fuller was also committed to group solidarity of a different kind.

## Notes

1. Edward A. Hoyt and Loriman S. Brigham, 'Glimpses of Margaret Fuller: The Greene Street School and Florence', *New England Quarterly*, 29, 1956, pp. 87–98; quotations pp. 90, 91 and 95.
2. Dale Spender, *Women of Ideas and What Men Have Done to Them: From Aphra Behn to Adrienne Rich*, London: Routledge & Kegan Paul, 1983 (hereafter Spender, *Women of Ideas*), p. 198.
3. Chevigny 1976a, p. 228; Higginson, p. 116.
4. *Life Without and Life Within*, p. 849.
5. *Summer on the Lakes*, pp. 46–7 and 85–6.
6. Welter, *Dimity Convictions*, p. 180.
7. Bernard Rosenthal, Introduction to Margaret Fuller, *Woman in the Nineteenth Century*, New York and London: W.W. Norton, 1977 (repr. of 1855 edn) (hereafter *Woman in the Nineteenth Century*), p. vii; Spender, *Women of Ideas*, p. 197.
8. Marie Olesen Urbanski, 'The Genesis, Form, Tone and Rhetorical Devices of *Woman in the Nineteenth Century*' (1973), repr. in Myerson (ed.), *Critical Essays*, pp. 268–80; *Woman in the Nineteenth Century*, p. 179.

9. Spender, *Women of Ideas*, p. 205.
10. *Woman in the Nineteenth Century*, p. 24–5.
11. Ibid, p. 37.
12. Ibid, pp. 169–70.
13. Ibid, pp. 38–43 and 93–5.
14. Ibid, p. 77.
15. Ibid, pp. 115–21.
16. Ibid, p. 174.
17. Ibid, p. 175.
18. *At Home and Abroad*, pp. 214–15.
19. Ibid, p. 232.
20. See Jane Rendall, *The Origins of Modern Feminism: Women in Britain, France and the United States, 1780–1860*, Basingstoke: Macmillan, 1985, pp. 277–85 and pp. 300–7.
21. Anthony, p. 81.
22. Chevigny 1976a, p. 210.

# 7 Socialism

Margaret Fuller's political conciousness, which has come to be praised by modern scholars for its unusual sensitivity to major historical developments in Europe, took some time to move from the abstract to the concrete. For all of her frustration with the ethereal qualities of Emerson and others of their transcendentalist friends it was only when she made the physical break from them, by moving to New York, that her emotional dissatisfaction was matched by more strongly stated political concerns. Similarly, it was only when she made the further physical break of moving to Europe that she began to develop a theoretically informed critique of American social and political development. It was also from Europe that she began to think seriously about the possibilities of the socialist transformation at which she had scoffed in the context of Brook Farm.

Placing a rough template over the development of Fuller's political ideas exposes the following broad developmental pattern. From her father she inherited a strong and well-informed respect for republican civic virtue, in particular the Roman model. In the last years of his life, at Groton, this had been reinforced by their reading together of Thomas Jefferson's correspondence. From this dialogue Fuller emerged with a vision of enlightened statesmanship, which informed much of her early writing (for example, the defence of Brutus). At this stage she established an ideal of individual virtue and leadership that sat well with the solipsistic tendencies of early romanticism and transcendentalism.

Thus it is not hard to see much of the ferment of social and political reformism of the 1830s and early 1840s passing Fuller by. At this stage, for example, she distrusted the abolitionists, for their partisan zeal and, more cerebrally, for their single-minded focus on the emancipation of the slaves. Francis Kearns, who has studied this aspect most closely, points to her rejection of the suggestion that one of the Boston 'Conversations' be dedicated to the subject. In December 1840 she wrote to Maria Weston Chapman, Treasurer of the Massachusetts Anti-Slavery Society, explaining her decision.

> The Abolition cause commands my respect as do all efforts to relieve and raise suffering human nature. The faults of the party are such as, it seems to me, must always be incident to the partizan spirit. All that was noble and pure in their zeal has helped us all. For the disinterestedness and constancy of many individuals among you I have a high respect. Yet my own path tends a different course and often leaves me quite ignorant what you are doing, as in the present instance of your Fair [the annual Massachusetts Anti- Slavery Fair]. . . .
>
> The late movements in your party have interested me more than those which had for their object the enfranchisement of the African only. Yet I presumed I should still feel sympathy with your aims only not with your measures. Yet I should like to be more fully acquainted with both. The late Convention I attended hoping to hear some clear account of your wishes as to religious institutions and the social position of women. But not only I heard nothing that pleased me, but no clear state-ment from any one.[1]

Those who have tried to establish from this and other state-ments that Fuller's political antennae were as sensitive as any of the more militant ladies who attended her 'Conversations', and that she was already placing abolitionism and other enthusiasms in context have set themselves a hard task.[2] An indication of the extent to which she shared the other transcendentalists' patrician disdain for social upheaval in the name of progress can be found in her reaction to Thomas Dorr's abortive rebellion against the restricted suffrage of the Rhode Island Constitution. Fuller had been in the state at the end of June 1842 when Dorr and leaders of his 'Suffrage Party' were captured by the state militia. In July she wrote to William Channing,

> I came into the very midst of the fuss, and tedious as it was at the time, I am glad to have seen it. I shall in future be able to believe real what I have read with a dim disbelief of such times and tendencies. There is, indeed, little good, little cheer in what I have seen: a city full of grown-up people as wild, as mischief-seeking, as full of prejudice, careless slander and exaggeration, as a herd of boys in the playground of the worst boarding-school. Women whom I have seen, as the domestic

cat, gentle, graceful, cajoling, suddenly showing the disposition, if not the force, of the tigress. I thought I appreciated the monstrous growths of rumour before, but I never did. The Latin poet [Virgil], though used to a court, has faintly described what I saw and heard often, in going the length of a street. It is astonishing what force, purity, and wisdom it requires for a human being to keep clear of falsehoods. These absurdities, of course, are linked with good qualities, with energy of feeling, and with a love of morality, though narrowed and vulgarized by the absence of the intelligence which should enlighten. I had the good discipline of trying to make allowance for those making none, to be charitable to their want of charity, and cool without being cold. But I don't know when I have felt such an aversion to my environment and prayed so earnestly day by day, — 'O, Eternal [,] purge from my inmost heart this hot haste about ephemeral trifles,' and 'keep back thy servant from presumptuous sins; let them not have dominion over me.'[3]

I have quoted the passage at length for several reasons, not least the contrast with her later passionate engagement with, and trust in, the demonstrations of the Roman crowd. It is also revealing for its glimmers of self-knowledge (trying to be 'cool without being cold') and the techniques Fuller uses to distance herself (for example, in Chevigny's words, she 'transcends the rebellion through reference to literature').[4] The key is the reliance on the individual 'human being' as a moral arbiter.

Throughout this period she wrote frequently to Channing (who also shared some of her early adventures in New York) trying to establish her critical point of view. There were some ironies to the stance she adopted (accusing Emerson, for example, of having 'faith in the Universal, but not in the individual man'), but the thrust of her concern was for an individual and a spiritual liberation. Channing chose to reflect this in a series of extracts from an important letter probably of late 1840, which survives only in the *Memoirs*. After deploring how '[since] the Revolution, there has been little, in the circumstances of this country to call out the higher sentiments', Fuller lays the blame almost equally on the 'vulgarity of a commercial aristocracy' and 'radicals' who have reacted to it.

Is this protest indiscriminating? are these opinions crude? do these proceedings threaten to sap the bulwarks on which men at present depend? I confess it all, yet I see in these men promise of a better wisdom than in their opponents. Their hope for man is grounded on his destiny as an immortal soul, and not as a mere comfort-loving inhabitant of earth, or as a subscriber to the social contract. It was not meant that the soul should cultivate the earth, but that the earth should educate and maintain the soul. Man is not made for society, but society is made for man. No institution can be good which does not tend to improve the individual.

After anticipating her later criticism of their associationist experiments ('Utopia it is impossible to build up. At least, my hopes for our race on this are more limited than those of most of my friends'), Fuller declares her sympathy for the 'Transcendental party'. 'They acknowledge in the nature of man an arbiter for his deeds, — a standard transcending sense and time, — and are in my view, the true utilitarians'. At this stage she was resolutely, although critically, on the side of the idealists against those who would insist on 'the material' in man.

Is it not the object of all philosophy, as well as of religion and poetry, to prevent its [materialism's] prevalance? Must not those who see most truly be ever making statements of the truth to combat this sluggishness, or wordliness? What else are sages, poets, preachers, born to do? Men go on an undulating course, — sometimes on the hill, sometimes in the valley. But he is only in the right who in the valley forgets not the hill-prospect, and knows in darkness that the sun will rise again. That is the real life which is subordinated to, not merged in, the ideal; he is only wise who can bring the lowest act of his life into sympathy with its highest thought.[5]

This exposition must have been close to that enjoyed by the ladies in Fuller's conversation classes, and goes some way towards explaining the criticism of those who found them politically naïve. In this genre the most famous example, and perhaps the least responsible, is the posthumous attack by Harriet Martineau in her *Autobiography*, quoted in almost every Fuller biography and relevant anthology. Martineau, who can only have heard about the events second hand, combined censure and frustration in almost equal measures.

> While Margaret Fuller and her adult pupils sat 'gorgeously dressed', talking about Mars and Venus, Plato and Goethe, and fancying themselves the elect of the earth in intellect and refinement, the liberties of the republic were running out as fast as they could go, at a breach which another sort of elect persons were devoting themselves to repair; and my complaint against the 'gorgeous' pedants was that they regarded their preservers as hewers of wood and drawers of water, and their work as a less vital one than the pedantic orations which were spoiling a set of well-meaning women in a pitiable way.[6]

Fuller's allies, from Higginson onwards, have fought back against this influential and effective piece of character assassination, citing the personal animus which had developed between the two women and identifying the participants in the class who on other afternoons were at the barricades themselves.[7] However, before the completion of *Woman in the Nineteenth Century* and her move to New York, it is a fair summary to define Fuller's political views as structured around ideals of moral individualism and leadership, and deeply sceptical about political organisation.

In the next phrase of her career, up to her departure for Europe, Fuller's hostility to political movements softened considerably. She embraced the abolitionist cause tentatively in *Summer in the Lakes*, unequivocally in *Woman in the Nineteenth Century* and actively in articles for the *Tribune*. Simultaneously, and largely under the influence of Greeley, one of whose enthusiasms this was, she began sympathetically to reappraise Fourier and the associationists. Finally, and for more than straightforward environmental reasons, she became a campaigner.

I have listed above some of Fuller's enthusiams while in New York, and commented upon their limitations. Taken together it is hard to characterise them as a major theoretical advance. None the less, they were important for adding a social and political dimension to her developing ideas about the literary and moral regeneration of America. Her review of a volume simply entitled *American Facts* 1845 gives some measure of the state of her mind at this stage, acutely conscious of American destiny, criticising her generation on largely moral grounds, and still searching for national leadership.

> We doubt not the destiny of our country — that she is to accomplish great things for human nature, and be the mother of a nobler race than the world has yet known. But she has been so false to the scheme made out at her nativity, that it is now hard to say which way that destiny points. We can hardly exhibit the true American facts without some idea of the real character of America. Only one thing seems clear — that the energy here at work is very great, though the men employed in carrying out its purposes may have generally no more individual ambition to understand those purposes, or cherish noble ones of their own, than the coral insect through whose restless working new continents are upheaved from the ocean's breast.

As in literature the test is at this stage a comparative one, based on a curious mixture of envy and suspicion of European achievement.

> But we look about in vain for traits as characteristic of what may be individually the character of the nation, as we can find at a glance in reference to Spain, England, France, or Turkey. America is as yet but a European Babe; some new ways and motions she has, consequent on a new position; but that soul that may shape her mature life scarce begins to know itself yet. One thing is certain; we live in a large place, no less morally than physically: woe to him who lives meanly here, and knows the exhibitions of selfishness and vanity as the only American facts.[8]

To return to my metaphor of the template, it was her first-hand experience in England, France, and most emphatically Italy, that moved Fuller's political consciousness into its third and most decisive phase. From Europe she reached a mature and positive appreciation of Fourier and the associationists, learned at first hand about the theory and practice of European republicanism and Italian nationalism, finally extending both beyond the mystical formulations of both Gioberti and Mazzini, and began work on a tantalising and elusive personal formulation which is likely to have linked social with sexual liberation, perhaps extending

Fourier rather than absorbing Marx.

The re-estimate of Fourier was not only a consequence of going to the source (she met not only Considérant, but also possibly Pierre Leroux, who had translated 'American Literature' for his *Revue Indépendante* and offered her a job) but also of her keen awareness of the French political scene. Writing her farewell letter to Paris for the *Tribune* in February 1847 she made explicit the political connections of a doctrine she had never really appreciated in the insular and self-satisfied confines of Brook Farm.

> While Louis Philippe lives, the gases, compressed by his strong grasp may not burst up to light; but the need of some radical measures of reform is not less strongly felt in France than elsewhere, and the time will come before long when such will be imperatively demanded. The doctrines of Fourier are making considerable progress, and wherever they spread, the necessity of some practical application of the precepts of Christ, in lieu of the mummeries of a worn-out ritual, cannot fail to be felt. The more I see of the terrible ills which infest the body politic of Europe, the more indignation I feel at the selfishness or stupidity of those in my own country who oppose an examination of these subjects — such as is animated by the hope of prevention.

Characteristically Fuller went on to confess the nature of her conversion; although '[the] mind of Fourier was, in many respects, uncongenial to mine. . . . his views were large and noble'. However, by the time she left France she was clearly prepared to give serious attention to the most radical doctrine available in general discourse about society.[9]

The example of France was also important in influencing the next of her personal political moves. In London and Paris she had been profoundly affected by the moral qualities and nationalistic fervour of Mazzini and Mickiewicz. Writing from Italy almost exactly a year later (March 1848), and a month after the first Italian uprising, she described her forecast coming true.

> The news of dethronement of Louis Philippe reached us just after the close of Carnival. It was just a year from my leaving Paris. I did not think, as I looked with such disgust on the

empire of sham he had established in France, and saw the soul of the people imprisoned and held fast as in an iron vice, that it would burst its chains so soon. Whatever be the result, France has done gloriously; she has declared that she will not be satisfied with pretexts while there are facts in the world, — that to stop her march is a vain attempt, through the onward path be dangerous and difficult. It is vain to cry, Peace! peace! when there is no peace.

By this stage the political and the social analyses are fully integrated as Fuller concludes her exhortation to readers in America in terms which are unambiguously socialist.

It would appear that the political is being merged in the social struggle: it is well. Whatever blood is to be shed, whatever altars cast down, those tremendous problems MUST be solved, whatever be the cost! That cost cannot fail to break many a bank, many a heart in Europe, before the good can bud again out of a mighty corruption. To you, people of America, it may perhaps be given to look on and learn in time for a preventive wisdom. You may learn the real meaning of the words FRATERNITY, EQUALITY: you may, despite the apes of the past who strive to tutor you, learn the needs of a true democracy. You may in time learn to reverence, learn to guard, the true aristocracy of a nation, the only real nobles, — the LABORING CLASSES.[10]

During the course of the next year, as she became more and more intimately involved in the development of the Italian and, specifically, Roman revolutions, Fuller overlaid this growing enthusiasm for socialist prospects with a detailed and sophisticated understanding of the Italian case. She and Ossoli shared republican newspapers from all over the country, and she corresponded and conversed with the leading figures, particularly in Milan and Florence. As a consequence her analysis of the unfolding situation — for example the gradual isolation of Pius IX and the limited prospects of French assistance to the Roman uprising — was ahead of many of her collaborators and certainly far ahead of any contemporary American commentator. Several elements stand out in this impressive body of committed journalism: her growing anti-clericalism (the extent to which she was initially prepared to give the Church the benefit of the doubt may have had something to do with respect for Ossoli's deeply held Catholicism), her recognition that the crowd had served to move the cause along (rather than hinder it, as in Dorr's rebellion), and her affectionate but ultimately damning estimate of Mazzini's vision and political goals. As she wrote to the *Tribune* celebrating his return from exile:

> He returns, like Wordsworth's great man, 'to see what he foresaw'. He will see his predictions accomplishing yet for a long time, for Mazzini has a mind far in advance of his times in general, and his nation in particular, — a mind that will be best revered and understood when the 'illustrious Gioberti' shall be remembered as a pompous verbose charlatan, with just talent enough to catch the echo from the advancing wave of his day, but without any true sight of the wants of man at this epoch. And yet Mazzini sees not all: he aims at political emancipation; but he sees not, perhaps would deny, the bearing of some events, which ever now begin to work their way. Of this more anon; but not today, nor in the small print of the Tribune. Suffice it to say, I allude to that of which the cry of Communism, the systems of Fourier, etc., are but forerunners.[11]

Fuller's brother Arthur confidently concluded his collection of her European journalisms in *At Home and Abroad* with a final letter dated 6 July 1849, satisfyingly wrapping up the story of the siege with the departure of Garibaldi, some praise for the work of Lewis Cass, and the promise to retire to mountains and reflect: 'let not my friends be surprised if they do not hear from me for some time'.[12] For well over a century this editorial act misled Fuller's biographers, including Chevigny in 1975. More recently Chevigny has returned to the *Tribune* archives to discover at least three further contributions, taking Fuller's comments up to February 1850. In these the themes of anticlericalism, popular uprising and unfinished business loom large. Chevigny also draws her own analysis of Fuller's reflections of the contemporary ideologies of class and gender together.

> We know that, in preparation of her book, Fuller was reading materials that lay beyond the Italian story. She was concerned both with the underground and feminist strand of Fourierism

which argued for sexual liberation, freedom from gender stereotyping and reshaping of the family, and with the case Louis Blanc made for worker's control of their labor. If she had established in her book a connection between these two early traditions of socialism, the loss of it is incalculably greater than is generally imagined. [13]

Ultimately, of course, modern speculation about the content and extent of completion of Fuller's most important manuscript is only a little more privileged in terms of evidence than that of the searchers for wreckage of the *Elizabeth* along the beaches of Fire Island. Our chief advantage is not so much additional evidence as the distance from which to read it. Fuller did not achieve and leave us anything like a final synthesis of her romanticism, her feminism and her socialism; nor, given the span of a normal working life, could we have necessarily expected it at the point where she died. Distance should have helped us at least to assess her work in its more and less integrated phases. In the next chapter I discuss why this has not generally been the case.

# Notes

1. Francis E. Kearns, 'Margaret Fuller and the Abolition Movement' (1964), repr. in Myerson (ed.), *Critical Essays*, pp. 247–58; *Letters*, II, pp. 197–8.
2. Higginson, pp. 122–9.
3. *Letter*, III, pp. 73–4.
4. Chevigny 1986, pp. 175–6.
5. *Letters*, II, pp. 108–10 and III, pp. 90–2.
6. Chevigny 1976a, p. 229.
7. Higginson, pp. 127–8.
8. *Life Without and Life Within*, pp. 108–9.
9. *At Home and Abroad*, pp. 205–6.
10. Ibid, pp. 305–6.
11. Ibid, p. 320.
12. Ibid, pp. 410–12.
13. Chevigny 1976a, p. 479; and 1986, pp. 192–3.

# Part III  The Reputation

*Margaret Fuller*

# 8 The *Memoirs*

Of all the posthumous 'appropriations' of Fuller's life and work, that effected by the editors of her so-called *Memoirs* — Emerson, Channing and Clarke — has proved the most durable, and the most sinister. From the rather hurried publication of the two volumes in 1852 (three in the London imprint) until the appearance of Mason Wade's anthology in 1941 (itself heavily dependent on the *Memoirs* for those sections he chose to reprint) it was virtually the only accessible source for Fuller's writings. In 1963 Perry Miller was also forced to acknowledge the *Memoirs* as 'the indispensable source book for the study of the life and mind of Margaret Fuller', in preparing his collection *Margaret Fuller: American Romantic*.[1] That the failures of this rapidly constructed (and somewhat reluctant) editorial team are now so transparent must not be allowed to disguise their success in protecting the good name of their subject for well over a century.

By all accounts the formation of the editorial team for the *Memoirs* went through a process of manoeuvring not dissimilar to that which made Fuller the first editor of *The Dial*. Her friends saw the necessity (and the market) for a memorial of this sort, but also appreciated the extent of the problems they had to overcome, not only in collecting together the disparate corpus of published and unpublished work but also in overcoming the hint of scandal. Sam Ward was one of the early retirements from the scene, while contributions apparently promised from Mazzini and the Brownings never appeared. In the end it was Emerson who supervised the rather odd arrangement of the volumes. Personal recollections from himself, Channing and Clarke serve as introductions to heavily edited selections from Fuller's journal entries, letters and extracts from books and articles, while other witnesses are called upon to fill particular gaps, including Emelyn Story on Fuller's 'marriage' and life in Rome during the siege.[2]

As modern scholarship has checked their work against the evidence of Fuller's manuscripts (and occasionally work she had previously published herself) the effects of the heavy editorial hand have become progressively clearer. Putting aside for a

91

moment the question of motive, it is possible to discern three main areas (two destructive, one 'creative') in which an undeclared set of editorial decisions has moulded and distorted the material.

Politically the triumvirate took the edge off both Fuller's growing radicalism and her linked readiness to be sceptical and free-thinking about religion. Morally they overemphasized the failures of her love-life before meeting Ossoli, correspondingly painted her as traditionally as they could (given some severe problems of evidence) in the roles of wife and mother, and throughout undermined or just suppressed any expression of romantic or sexual feeling which they felt might cause offence. Constructively they, like some of the modern scholars discussed above, were concerned to impose some order or unity on the story. The chosen device was that of the Greek tragedy, with the inevitable price paid for hubris or stepping outside of the acceptable bounds of personal aspiration. No premonitory passage about early death or fate escapes comment, while the final selection before description of her final voyage is probably the high point of the genre:

> I have a vague expectation of some crisis, — I know not what. But it has long seemed, that, in the year 1850, I should stand on a plateau in the ascent of life, where I should be allowed to pause for a while, and take more clear and commanding views than ever before. Yet my life proceeds as regularly as the fates of a Greek tragedy, and I can but accept the pages as they turn.[3]

It must also be assumed that her family, particularly her brothers Richard and Arthur, colluded in the definition of these standards. Certainly Arthur's own editorial work (praised by Miller as more accurate) exhibits the same three themes in equal measure.[4]

Space does not permit more than a few examples of the editorial process at work. One which joins the religious and sexual themes is the version prepared for the *Memoirs* of a fanciful letter Fuller wrote to Beethoven after hearing a concert of his work in November 1843. The manuscript includes the following passages showing Fuller perhaps approaching the zenith of her frustration with life in Boston and the inadequacies of transcendentalism as a living faith:

> But thou, oh blessed master! dost answer all my questions, and make it my privilege to be. Like a humble wife to the sage or poet, it is my triumph that I can understand, can receive thee wholly, like a mistress I arm thee for the fight, like a young daughter, I tenderly bind thy wounds. Thou art to me beyond compare, for thou art all I want. No heavenly sweetness of Jesus, no many-leaved Raphael, no golden Plato, is anything to me, compared with thee.

And

> If thou wouldst take me wholly to thyself. I am lost in this world where I sometimes meet angels, but of a different star from mine. Forgive me that I love thou who cannot love me. Even so does thy spirit call upon, plead with all spirits. But thou dost triumph and bring them all in.
>
> Master! I have this summer envied the oriole which had ever a swinging nest in the high bough. I have envied the least flower that came to seed, though that seed were strown to the wind. But I envy none when I am with thee. Tonight I had no wish for thee: it was long since we had met. I did not expect to feel again. I was so very cold; tears had fallen; but they were Hamlet tears of speculation. Thy touch has made me again all human. O save and give me to myself and thee.

Here are the corresponding passages prepared for the *Memoirs*, probably by Channing, who Chevigny estimates did the bulk of this kind of blue-pencilling:

> But thou, O blessed master! dost answer all my questions, and make it my priviledge to be. Like a humble wife to the sage or poet, it is my triumph that I can understand and cherish thee: like a mistress, I arm thee for the fight: like a daughter, I tenderly bind thy wounds. Thou art to me beyond all compare, for thou art all I want. No heavenly sweetness of saint or martyr, no many-leaved Raphael, no golden Plato, is anything to me, compared with thee.

> If thou wouldst take me wholly to thyself — ! I am lost in this world, where I sometimes meet angels, but of a different star

from mine. Even so does thy spirit plead with all spirits. But thou dost triumph, and will bring them all in.

Master, I have this summer envied the oriole, which had ever a swinging nest in the high bough. I have envied the least flower than came to seed, though that seed were strown to the wind. But I envy none when I am with thee.

The most important feature is not so much the omissions (still less the finicky and inconsistent amendment of Fuller's punctuation), although these do reduce the powerful sense of despair and abandonment in the original. More corrosive are the changes: replacing the blasphemous allusion to Jesus as just another romantic hero, and smoothing out any hint of sexual desire.[5]

The most comprehensive charge-sheet of this kind is probably included in Chevigny's article on 'The Long Arm of Censorship: Myth-making in Margaret Fuller's Time and Our Own' (1976). Accepting that the political judgements made by the editors could be excused partially by ignorance (the evidence was just not readily available for how far Fuller's movement towards socialism had developed by her death) or the distractions of domestic conflict in the decade before the Civil War, her chief concern is this 'persistent effort — by omission or addition — to *make over* the moral image of Margaret Fuller, especially the two areas of sacred or profane emotion, or religion and passion'. Among the most telling examples is the editorial decision to halt an extract from a manuscript just before this arresting estimate of her relationship with Ossoli.

Our relation covers only a part of my life, but I do not perceive that it interferes with anything I ought to have or be: I do not feel anyway constrained or limited or that I have made any sacrifice. Younger I might, because I should have been exposed to love some other in a way that might give him pain, but I do not feel apprehensive of that. There is more danger for him, as he is younger than I; if he should, I shall do all that this false state of society permits to give him what freedom he may need.[6]

Other contemporary feminist critics are less understanding than Chevigny. For Dale Spender, Fuller's *Memoirs* constitute one of the most persuasive cases in her long essay *Women of Ideas: And*

*What Men Have Done to Them* (1982):

> So blatant is the misrepresentation of Margaret Fuller in the authoritative records, and so readily has this misrepresentation been accepted (or excused where exposed) that it is possible to dismiss completely any claims of objectivity or veracity, or even fairness, and to argue that male fantasies abound in what we have been led to believe are unchallengeable stories. The image constructed of Margaret Fuller suggests that men may invent anything they choose and pass it off as truth. We are worse than gullible if we take their truths at face value particularly when they portray women negatively.[7]

Spender is particularly scathing about the excuse put forward by Perry Miller after his own confession of reliance on the *Memoirs* and their editors:

> These three had not only a deep affection for her but also manly respect for her intellect and courage. They made a gallant effort to treat her as a Romantic heroine, to tell all the truth and to show in their tone that they were men of the world.
> Unfortunately their standards of scholarship were those of their age, of a culture in which there had not yet emerged professional canons. It is not so much that they suppressed unpleasant passages, and it must be said on their behalf that they were not, where they might have been, censorious.[8]

Self-serving as this comment might seem (and Spender, Urbanski and others have shown how in his lengthy Foreword to the collection Miller himself reflects many of the prejudices of Fuller's male friends) it does hint at a more important point. As literary critics Emerson, Channing and Clarke not only lacked the modern respect for scholarly apparatus as Spender deplores, they were also wedded to and attempting to live up to a theory of criticism which they had learned from Margaret Fuller to a very significant extent. For her the critic should strive to get behind the details of the text itself, and even of the author's life, to the symbolic value of the work and the 'character' of the author. On one level this meant overcoming the 'merely reproductive' role of the critic to approach the 'apprehensive' and 'comprehensive' levels recommended in her 'Short Essay on Critics' (discussed on page 60). On another it is to 'estimate relations and perceive enduring value. As she wrote on Turner's pictures in comparison with those of the French Romantics: 'Art can only be truly Art by presenting an adequate outward symbol of some fact in the interior life. But then it *is* a symbol that Art seeks to prevent, and not the fact itself.'[9]

There can be little doubt that Emerson, Channing and Clarke were self-consciously creating and burnishing a symbol, and one which they felt warranted by what they understood of Fuller's interior life. Their frequent disclaimers about excisions make this point unselfconsciously and render Spender's conspiracy theory naïve. Take, for example, Clarke's introduction to his selection on 'Friendship':

> In giving some account of her in these relations, there is only the alternative of a prudent reserve which omits whatever is liable to be misunderstood, or a frank utterance which confides in the good sense and right feeling of the reader. By the last course, we run the risk of allowing our friend to be misunderstood; but by the first we make it certain that the most important part of her character shall not be understood at all.

It is only a little further into the selection that the censor raises his head: 'So that, in touching on these private relations we must be everywhere "bold", yet not "too bold"'.[10]

Given that the editorial intention was to establish the symbolic value of Fuller's life, and that her life has today such a starkly different resonance, how did the three get it so wrong? There are several possible reasons, most of which cohere around the unsatisfactory nature of their personal relationships with their subject.

In the first place they, unlike Mazzini, Mickiewicz and in his own way, Ossoli, were unable to accept her equality. Emerson writes revealingly about the failure of the original conception of the work as 'Margaret and her Friends': 'But, on trial, that form proved impossible, and it only remained that the narrative, like a Greek tragedy, should suppose the chorus always on the stage, sympathising and sympathised with by the queen of the scene'.[11] The failure was not only one of form. In their personal contributions each of the editors displays a simultaneous attraction to and repulsion from Fuller and her character. Personally, they established the myth of her prickliness and arrogance, and ensured that she, like prominent feminists from every age, suffered from an extended debate about her physical attractiveness. Critically the outcome is a series of judgements that fluctuate wildly between praise and disparagement, rarely able to control a measured qualification of either.

Emerson, for example, developed a thesis about her unchannelled power as an intellect and a personality. He is responsible for the anecdote which has her declaring: 'I now know all the people worth knowing in America, and I find no intellect comparable to my own', as well as the characterisation of 'a rather mountainous ME'. In assessing her work in his own area of specialisation — the poetic quality of natural phenomena — the dismissal is lofty and cruel.

> She paid homage to rocks, woods, flowers, rivers and the moon. She spent a good deal of time outdoors, sitting, perhaps, with a book in some sheltered recess commanding a landscape. She watched by day and by night, the skies and the earth, and believed she knew all their expressions. She wrote in her journal, or in her correspondence, a series of 'moonlights,' in which she seriously attempts to describe the light and scenery of successive nights of the summer moon. Of course her raptures must appear sickly and superficial to an observer, who with equal feeling, had better powers of observation.[12]

This kind of putdown, coupled with the insistent editorial leitmotif that Fuller's powers lay more in conversation than writing (Clarke writes that '[our] friend was well aware that her *forte* was in conversation'; Emerson that 'all these powers and accomplishments found their best and only adequate channel in her conversation'), led the editors away from what is now regarded as her more original and creative work: *Woman in the Nineteenth Century* and the Italian dispatches.[13] This was their Margaret Fuller, or at least the one they were most comfortable with. They were not to know just how influential their version was to be.

# Notes

1. Mason Wade (ed.), *The Writings of Margaret Fuller*, New York: Viking Press, 1941; Miller (ed.), *Margaret Fuller*, p. 317
2. Blanchard, pp. 339–40; Anthony, pp. 208–9.
3. *Memoirs*, III, p. 315.
4. Arthur B. Fuller, 'Preface' to *Woman in the Nineteenth Century*, pp. 5–10.
5. Chevigny 1976a, pp. 61–9; *Memoirs*, I, pp. 312–14.
6. Chevigny 1976b, pp. 451–6.
7. Spender, *Women of Ideas*, p. 201; see also Marie Mitchell Olsen Urbanski, 'Margaret Fuller: Feminist Writer and Revolutionary', in Dale Spender (ed.), *Feminist Theories: Three Centuries of Women's Intellectual Traditions*, Shoreditch: Women's Press, 1983, pp. 75–89.
8. *Margaret Fuller, American Romantic*, p. 317
9. Papers on Literature and Art, pp. 1–8; *At Home and Abroad*, p. 198.
10. *Memoirs*, I, pp. 89 and 92.
11. Ibid, p. 273.
12. *Memoirs*, II, pp. 1, 3 and 42–3.
13. *Memoirs*, I, pp. 136–7.

# 9 Literary Representations

The main critical effect of the *Memoirs* was to entrench a view of Fuller as having failed as a writer. By overemphasising the quality of her conversation and personal communication, as well as judging harshly (and not always unreasonably) those areas in which she was demonstrably weakest (like the pastoral and poetry), the editors distracted attention from her more powerful and lasting work. They also exhibited in microcosm three types of reaction that soon became standard: hostile dismissal, occasional grudging admiration, and indifference to her work as opposed to her life.

The first is the easiest to characterise and exemplify, although the aggression with which it was expressed is often arresting. Fuller's own critical practice and conclusions made enemies, who, directly and by proxy, were not slow to react. The most famous riposte was that of James Russell Lowell, who deeply resented Fuller's low estimate not only of himself but also of Longfellow in her 'American Literature'. Longfellow she had declared to be 'artificial and imitative', and Lowell 'absolutely wanting in the true spirit and tone of poesy'. Lowell took his revenge in the 'Miranda' section of his 'Fable for Critics' published in 1848.

> She will take an old notion, and make it her own
> By saying it o'er in her sibylline tone,
> Or persuade you 'tis something tremendously deep,
> By repeating it so as to put you to sleep;
> And she may well defy any mortal to see through it,
> When once she has mixed up her infinite *me* through it,
> There is one thing she swears is her own single right,
> It is native and genuine — namely her spite;
> Though, when acting as censor, she privately blows
> A censer of vanity 'neath her own nose. . . .
>
> Miranda meanwhile has succeeded in drawing
> Up into a corner, in spite of their striving,
> A small flock of terrified victims, and there,

> With a I-turn-the-crank-of-the-Universe air
> And a tone which, at least to *my* fancy appears
> Not so much to be entering as boxing your ears,
> Is unfolding a tale (of herself, I surmise,
> For 'tis dotted as thick as a peacock's with I's) . . .[1]

The posthumously published verdict by Nathaniel Hawthorne was more savage but less easy to explain. Fuller had praised his work, calling him in the *Tribune* 'the best writer of the day', and had been close to him and his wife Sophia Peabody. Leaving aside the literary uses he made of her character, in which way she suffered like most of his friends, it is clear from their journals that while both were alive they enjoyed a healthy respect for each other. Speculation about his change of heart is rife; Chevigny reckons that the socially conventional Hawthorne could not cope with her combination of 'sexual honesty with intellectual activity and political commitment in Rome', while there is also evidence that at one stage he felt Sophie (his 'little wife') to be falling under her spell.

The denunciation of Fuller's hypocrisy and lack of originality which Hawthorne's son Julian included in the second edition of his father's *Italian Notebooks* in 1884 (Sophia had omitted it from her earlier selection of 1871) was unexpectedly harsh. Writing in 1858 about a visit from the sculptor Mozier (who turns up in almost all of these American records of life in mid-nineteenth-century Rome), he moves from gossip about Ossoli ('in short, half an idiot, and without any pretensions to be a gentleman') to an estimate of Fuller's character.

> But she was a woman anxious to try all things, and fill up her experience in all directions; she had a strong and coarse nature, too, which she had done her utmost to refine, with infinite pains, but which of course could only be superficially changed. The solution of the riddle lies in this direction; nor does one's conscience revolt at the idea of thus solving it; for — at least this is my own experience — Margaret has not left, in the heart and minds of those who knew her, any deep witness of her integrity and purity. She was a great humbug; of course with much talent, and much moral reality, or else she could not have been so great a humbug. But she had stuck herself full of borrowed qualities, which she chose to provide herself with,

but which had no root in her.

After reporting Mozier's 'certain knowledge' that the history of the Roman Revolution never existed, Hawthorne moves to the heart of his indictment: 'there appears to have been a total collapse in poor Margaret, morally and intellectually; and tragic as the catastrophe was, Providence was, after all, kind in putting her, and her clownish husband, and their child, on board that fated ship'. Her pretensions to 'moral excellence', by which he and Sophia could, if they admitted it, claim earlier to have been dazzled had proved to be flawed: 'by and by this rude old potency stirred itself, and undid all her labor in the twinkling of an eye. On the whole, I do not know but I like her the better for it, — the better, because she proved herself a very woman, after all, and fell as the weakest of her sisters might'.[2]

Writing his biography of Fuller in 1890, and thereby placing a small landmark on the road to her rehabilitation (he was bold enough to call her 'the best literary critic whom America has yet seen'), Higginson placed Lowell's attack in the category of 'tomahawk' criticism, where literary judgements inspired personal attacks. It is obviously hard to classify Hawthorne in such unambiguous terms, but there were a few among her immediate contemporaries who were able to develop anything like an objective assessment of her importance. An honourable exception to the general rule was Edgar Allan Poe, despite his resentment at having been omitted from 'American Literature' and his fellow-feeling for the slighted Lowell. He praised *Summer on the Lakes*, although chiefly for its 'conventional quality', and produced a rare appreciation of her achievement in *Woman in the Nineteenth Century*. For him, it was 'a book which few women in the country could have written, and no woman in the country would have published, with the exception of Miss Fuller'. Praising its 'independence' and 'unmitigated radicalism', he is also able to identify weaknesses (in the use of metaphor and analogy, for example, as well as passages of 'excessive subjectiveness') without using them as a case for dismissal.[3]

The general problem was, of course, that expressed by the scholars who have treated Fuller's critical reception in the decades after her death: the evidence of the life loomed larger than that of the work. Joel Myerson writes 'from the start, critics

reviewed Fuller more often than they did her work'.[4] Frances
Barbour reaches a similar conclusion in her analysis of the British
reception of the *Memoirs*: 'It was Margaret Fuller Ossoli, wife and
mother, not Margaret Fuller, woman of letters who interested
English critics in 1852'.[5]

The bulk of such work was predictably hostile, while even
those more favourably inclined also failed to escape from the
personalism of the trend and hence underlined rather than modi-
fied the emerging 'Margaret-Myth'. Henry James is a case in
point. His memoir, *William Wetmore Story and his Friends*, published
in 1903, shows him to have been clearly moved by her character
and her achievement, but progressively entrapped by each of the
main features of the myth.

James asks himself the question '*why* she may, to any such
degree, be felt as haunting?' His answers include her 'identity' as
'the talker, the moral improvisatrice', her role in youth as 'a
sparkling fountain to the other thirsty young', her having been
'incurably bitten' by Rome ('the wolf of the Capitol') and the
unsuspected 'underplot' of her marriage and child. He also spices
his account with the images of the 'New England Corinne' and
'the somewhat angular Boston sybil'. 'All of which, the free
lines overscaling the unlikely material, is doubtless why the
Margaret-ghost, as I have ventured to call it, still unmistakably
walks the old passages.'[6]

By this time the Margaret-ghost also had some thinly-
disguised vicarious incarnations. It is more than likely that James
drew upon her for several of his characters; certainly there are
echoes in Isabel Archer in *Portrait of a Lady* (1881) and Olive
Chancellor in *The Bostonians* (1886). The same model is claimed
for Olive Wendell Holmes' *Elsie Venner* (1861). But the most
famous, and least subtle appropriations are those of Hawthorne,
for Zenobia in the *Blithedale Romance* (1852) and Maria in the
*Marble Faun* (1860).

As Chevigny and others have shown, each of these characteris-
ations has highlighted a distorted view of Fuller, and acted
simultaneously to suppress her work and sharpen her caricature.
Hawthorne's elegy for Zenobia, after her disgraceful liaison with
the foreigner Westevelt (a name taken from the list of victims
from the *Elizabeth*) and her suicide by drowning, can stand as
representative of the kind of partiality thus inspired: 'It was a

woeful thought that a woman of Zenobia's diversified capacity should have fancied herself irretrievably defeated on the broad battlefield of life, and with no refuge, save 'to fall on her own sword, merely because Love had gone against her'.[7]

Critical and literary contributions to the 'Margaret-Myth' — of a talented and idiosyncratic but failed individual, redeemed temporarily by love and by political enthusiasm but unable appropriately to connect with her time — continue well into the twentieth century. Even the more sympathetic of her biographers — Julia Ward Howe in 1884, Anthony in 1922, Margaret Bell in 1930, Mason Wade in 1940, Madeleine Stern in 1942, and Faith Chipperfield in 1957 — in correcting the excesses of the editors of the *Memoirs* (on whom they invariably depend for much of their primary material) have generally assisted the perpetuation of the myth rather than its exposure. In this context Chipperfield's prologue and epilogue to *In Quest of Love*, imagining the thoughts in Fuller's mind as the *Elizabeth* breaks up, takes on a deep ironic quality:

The heart, the heart!
Is it not strange that no biographer has searched the story of Margaret Fuller's heart?
Is it not time, after a hundred years, to forget the Margaret Fuller of Victorian legend and remember the Margaret Fuller who lived and longed for love?[8]

Chipperfield was writing after a century of literary and critical appropriation that had attempted to do little else but search for Margaret Fuller's heart, condemning her to a fate from which it has taken modern feminist analysis to rescue her.

# Notes

1. *Papers on Literature and Art*, p. 132; Chevigny 1976a, pp. 163–5.
2. *Papers on Literature and Art*, p. 143; Chevigny 1976a, pp. 416–19.
3. Higginson, pp. 290–1 and 216; Chevigny 1976a, pp. 162, 184 and 232–3.
4. Myerson (ed.), *Critical Essays*, p. viii.
5. Frances Barbour, 'Margaret Fuller and the British Reviewers', *New England Quarterly*, 9, December 1936, pp. 618–25; Blanchard, p. 340.
6. Myerson (ed.), *Critical Essays*, pp. 131–2.
7. Nathaniel Hawthorne, *The Blithedale Romance*, Harmondsworth: Penguin, 1986, p. 241.
8. Faith Chipperfield, *In Quest of Love: The Life and Death of Margaret Fuller*, New York: Coward McCann, 1957, pp. 19–20, 298–9.

# 10 Fuller and Modern Feminism

This section begins from the premise that it is understandable and reasonable for historians and literary critics with feminist convictions to search for female individuals in the past who can act as powerful role models for contemporary feminist action. These individuals become a resource; in a post-structuralist sense their lives become texts, which can be read and interpreted in different contexts — to the extent that, like other texts, they can be stripped of their original contextual moorings. Fuller's rescue from the legacy of the editors of the *Memoirs*, chiefly effected by committed feminist scholars, is something of a test-case of the strengths and weaknesses of a methodology which incorporates such didactic and quasi-political purposes. There are several common themes in modern writing about notable women of earlier generations, each of which has been used in connection with Fuller's life and work with at least potentially distorting effect. Four can be singled out.

The first theme is prescience or presentism. By this I mean an exaggerated emphasis on the way in which the subject's life and work can be made to resonate in a contemporary context, as well as an underemphasis on those aspects not helpful in this way. Margaret Allen, for example, begins her study by declaring: 'She was born not only far ahead of *her* time, but even ahead of our time'. Similarly, but without the specifically feminist purpose, Joseph Diess begins *The Roman Years* by reflecting that 'no other American woman of any generation is so well worth recalling — not for her sake, but for ours'.[1]

Another such filter is perhaps best summed up in the feminist slogan 'the personal is the political', coined originally by Sara Evans. Female contributors to social development are marked on a different score-card from their male counterparts. This score-card emphasises individuality, self-awareness and personal fulfilment. To quote another of Fuller's modern biographers, Paula Blanchard: 'she should be remembered for what she was rather than what she did'. There is a particularly acute corollary to 'the personal is the political', in the emphasis on suffering, physical as well as mental. As Allen states: 'She may have thought like a man, but she hurt like a woman'.[2]

Neurastheniac invalidism and its treatment is a powerful element in the feminist case about the suppression of female originality and creativity in the nineteenth century.[3] Much has been made, correctly, of Fuller's health: her migraines, nose-bleeds, and curvature of the spine which brought her from time to time close to total incapacity. Even from this distance it is hard to avoid the conclusion that many of the problems were psychosomatic. What analyses of this type tend to overlook is that 'nervous sickness' in mid-nineteenth-century America was not exclusively and may not have even been predominantly a female problem. A good number of middle-class males as well as females were affected by it, and for many of the same reasons. The difference lay more in some aspects of its treatment, and more importantly in expectations of the patients of different sexes. For a classic case, almost contemporaneous with Fuller, contrast the experiences of Henry James' sister Alice and brother William. The latter recovered from a decade of crippling self-doubt and went on to preach the power of the individual will to overcome almost any obstacle; the former became one of the most celebrated (and certainly one of the most self-aware) invalids of her generation.[4]

Thirdly, there is a problem I would like to call univalence, or more crudely 'giving the benefit of the doubt'. The battle between Emerson and Fuller was a clash of two gigantic egos, often reflected as his head versus her heart. Among her judgemental words to him after the crisis over friendship, pointed up by Allen, were: 'You are intellect — but I am life'.[5] What is questionable in several feminist accounts is the allowance made for her weaknesses but not for his, the a priori assumption that her arguments were more sincere, and the attribution to him of responsibility for their failure. This is not to call into question any of the overwhelming evidence about Emerson's insecure and patronising attitude to women, but rather to query the value of such staged or loaded contests, whatever the other commitments of the investigator. I appreciate that it may reflect rebalancing of an historical prejudice, but, in doing so, so many of the arguments can become circular. She failed because he succeeded, he failed in succeeding.

Finally, there is the hagiographic emphasis on the sudden enlightenment, the conversion, or rescue of the subject, whether into the Church, into socialism or into sisterhood. Fuller has been the victim of some rather crude analyses of this sort, by authors of both sexes. There is, for example, something faintly embarrassing nowadays about Mason Wade's overtly Freudian account of Fuller's simultaneous experience of sexual and vocational fulfilment in Rome. Other biographers locate the point of enlightenment differently according to their particular interests. For Anne Rose it is the conversion experience of 1831 because it led her to transcendentalism. For Blanchard it was the discovery of the slums of New York which led her to 'social consciousness'. For Chevigny it was the discovery of Italian republicanism that led her to socialism.[6]

More positively, Fuller's life can be seen to fit into three major historiographical themes in nineteenth-century American social history, each of which represents an achievement of distinctively feminist scholarship.

Fuller's dilemmas as an example of what Barbara Welter terms 'the cult of true womanhood' when trying to explain some of the dynamics within her family before and after her father's death were discussed in Chapter 1. Her eventual escape from such an idealised female role tells us much about contemporary social pressures.

There is a subtle connection between Welter's sociological analysis and a broader cultural hypothesis put forward by Ann Douglas about the feminisation of culture in Victorian America. As the century moved on, articulate middle-class women were able to use the ideal role they had inherited to influence and set aspects of the cultural agenda. Fuller's concerns and career serve for her as a vital counter-indication. In Douglas' own words:

One could argue that the logical antagonist of Calvinism was a fully humanistic, historically-minded romanticism. Exponents of such romanticism appeared in mid nineteenth century America — one thinks particularly of Margaret Fuller and Herman Melville — but they were rare. In America, for economic and social reasons, Calvinism was largely defeated by an anti-intellectual sentimentalism purveyed by men and women whose victory did not achieve their first goals; America lost its male-dominated theological tradition without gaining a comprehensive feminism or an adequately modernised religious sensibility.[7]

Douglas' thesis is itself controversial with feminist scholars, who object to its apparently limited definition of the feminine, and in particular her exclusion of female (and feminist) contributions to political dissent in the tradition of the abolitionists. However, it is hard to argue against the conclusion that explicit cultural acceptance of a 'separate sphere' for women and their influence gave identity and a kind of power but also marginality in the wider political arena. Again Fuller's extraordinary career can be used to measure the limits of acceptable dissent from a broad historical pattern.

My third example uses Fuller neither as aberration nor as a figure on the margin. I refer to the work concerning relations between women of the same and adjacent generations inaugurated by William Taylor and Christopher Lasch in their essay on 'Sorority and Family', but carried forward and transformed by Carroll Smith-Rosenberg. Smith-Rosenberg's essay on 'The Female World of Love and Ritual' which appeared in the first number of the journal *Signs* (1975) has proved one of the most influential pieces of work in American women's history over the last decade. In it she analyses the correspondence and diaries of women and men in thirty-five families, representing 'a broad range of the American middle class' between the 1860s and 1880s. The effect is to reveal 'a female world of varied and yet highly structured relationships' as 'an essential aspect of American society'. 'These relationships ranged from the supportive love of sisters, through the enthusiasms of adolescent girls, to sensual avowals of love by mature women. It was a world in which men made but a shadowy appearance'.[8]

Fuller, although not centrally represented in this essay, is a magnificent demonstration of its main theses. Her correspondence is studded with example of the support network in action. This early (1830) letter to Almira Barlow, a friend from childhood and another potential model for Zenobia (she lived with her children at Brook Farm after separating from her husband), is typical.

Many things have happened since I echoed your farewell laugh. Elizabeth [Randall] and I have been fully occupied. She has cried a great deal, fainted a good deal and played the harp most of all. I have neither fertilized the earth with my tears, edified its inhabitants by my own delicacy of constitution, nor wakened its echoes to my own harmony — yet some things have I achieved in my own soft feminine style. I hate glare, thou knowest, and have hitherto successfully screened my virtues therefrom. I have made several garments fitted for the wear of American youth; I have written six letters, and received a correspondent number; I have read one book, — a piece of poetry entitled 'Two Agonies'. by M.A. Bourne, (pretty caption, is it not?) and J.J. Knapp's trial; I have given advice twenty times, — I have taken it once; I have gained two friends, and recovered two; I have felt admiration four times, — horror once, and disgust twice; I have been on a journey, and showed my penetration in discovering the beauties of Nature through a thick and never-lifted shroud of rain . . .[9]

Fuller confused, unsettled and quite simply scared many of the men she met. Edgar Allan Poe divided humanity into three classes: men, women, and Margaret Fuller. She never sought this effect, but she did refuse to make compromises. In contrast, her relationships with other women, including those you might have expected to have been overawed by her, were invariably warm. The record of her correspondence shows her at the centre of many of the axes of mutual respect, support and love of the type identified by Smith-Rosenberg — frequently giving advice, occasionally receiving it, but dealing with her friends with a mixture of wit, concern and sensitivity that should not be diminished by the fact that so much of her experience was painfully different from theirs. In this third context she can be shown as contributing to, rather than distancing herself from a generalised social phenomenon; perhaps because, of the three I have mentioned, it contained the most liberating possibilities.

One major conclusion from this survey is that feminist scholars have not fully overcome the potentially distorting effect of a concentration on Fuller's personality which they find distracting and unacceptable in much of the work of their predecessors. Indeed several of the interpretative themes upon which they regularly rely (presentism, personalism, revaluation and 'conversion') are hard to sustain without a primary focus on the subject's personality and the author's reactions to it. Where Fuller has been used in the wider context of feminist social and cultural history the outcomes seem more securely grounded, both in assessing the significance of her life and the choices she made, and in evaluating her work.

Biography has, however, been a potent force in feminist analysis, notwithstanding its difficulties. Almost a decade after completing her major study of Fuller, Chevigny wrote movingly about the subjective and objective dilemmas inherent in her relationship with her subject. Focusing in particular on Fuller's isolated attempts at autobiography, she identifies both projects (Fuller's autobiography and her own biography of Fuller) as acts of parental reparation: 'My efforts to understand her were rooted not only in my desire for vicarious self-knowledge, but also in a desire to know a precursor in ways I could not know my own mother'. The critical problem is to balance this intimate level of involvement with a subject (Chevigny calls it 'identification') with the distance and objectivity that are regarded as prerequisites for scholarly analysis (which she calls 'separation'). As she observes, 'some of our deeper motives will emerge only when the work is done'.

Chevigny's answer is at least in part to reject the dichotomy. Against the canons of traditional (male) scholarship she is able to make two powerful points: first that the 'universal truths' about female experience at which it could be said to be aiming are 'failures to come to terms with historical specificity'; and secondly, that the very processes of 'emotional identification' are themselves 'potentially analytical'.[10]

But is it a problem that feminist biography should so regularly be advocacy, even when it is a subtly shaded and qualified as by Chevigny? I have already referred to the claimed contemporaneity of Margaret Allen's *The Achievement of Margaret Fuller*, which concludes with a defiant score-line: 'She was easily the equal of her contemporaries Emerson and Thoreau. . . . but the conditions of her life were more difficult'. Paula Blanchard's much more detailed biography is equally explicit: 'This book is an attempt to view Margaret Fuller's life through the eyes of another woman, living in the 1970s with an awareness of the questions raised about women in the past decade. In other words, this is not an unbiased biography, though I have tried to do justice to the full variety and subtlety of Margaret's personality'.[11]

Just how historically contingent this approach can become is well illustrated by Fuller's relationship with Harriet Martineau, a feminist with at least an equal status in the canonical history of women's liberation. Their careers have some precise parallels: early educational demands, illness overcome, fame and respect for their social commentary. Martineau's criticism of Fuller's political timidity, as reflected in the topics and style of the 'Conversations', has already been noted. Ironically these faults were later compounded for Martineau by Fuller's social recklessness, precisely the qualities for which she is now admired: 'All this might have been spared, and a world of good effected, if she had found her heart a dozen years sooner, and in America instead of Italy. It is the most grievous loss I have almost ever known in private history — the deferring of Margaret Fuller's married life so long'.[12]

# Notes

1. Allen 1979, p. xii; Deiss, p. vi.
2. Blanchard, p. 342; Allen 1979, p. 136.
3. See Barbara Ehrenreich and Deidre English, *For Her Own Good: 150 Years of the Experts' Advice to Women*, London: Pluto Press, 1979, pp. 91–126.
4. See Howard M. Feinstein, *Becoming William James*, Ithaca and London: Cornell U. Press, 1984, *passim*.
5. *Letters*, III, pp. 209–10; Allen 1979, pp. 25–44.
6. Mason Wade, *Margaret Fuller: Whetstone of Genius*, New York: Viking Press, 1940; Blanchard, pp. 229 and 275; Anne C. Rose, *Transcendentalism as a Social Movement*, New Haven and London: Yale U. Press, 1981 (hereafter Rose), p. 59; Chevigny 1976a, pp. 366–97.
7. Ann Douglas, *The Feminization of American Culture*, New York, Knopf, 1977, pp. 12–13 and 259–88.
8. William R. Taylor and Christopher Lasch, 'Two Kindred Spirits: Sorority and Family in New England, 1839–46', *New England Quarterly*, 1963, pp. 23–41; Caroll Smith-Rosenberg, *Disorderly Conduct: Visions of Gender in Victorian America*, New York and Oxford: Oxford U. Press, 1985, pp. 53–75.
9. *Letters*, I, pp. 93, 171.
10. Chevigny 1983, *passim*.
11. Allen 1979, p. 178; Blanchard, p. 2.
12. *Harriet Martineau's Autobiography* (1877), quoted in Chevigny 1976a, p. 230.

# 11 Postscript

Towards the end of her stay in Italy Fuller wrote to her sister Ellen in terms echoing her earlier estimate of George Sand: 'for bad or good I acted out my character'.[1] The kind of psychological determinism which this conclusion has encouraged has, I think, been more damaging than helpful in the historiographical record of commentary and scholarship about Fuller. The temptations of a psychological explanation of almost every phase of Fuller's career are immense and in seeking to avoid them as far as possible this account represents a conscious effort to rebalance the interpretative record.

The question of Fuller's character is, however, an important one, which must be faced by a male writer presenting views about a woman whose life has been of particular and personal importance to women who have studied it. (I suspect that Fuller herself would have been more sympathetic to me in this dilemma than some of her modern female advocates.)

I do not find in Fuller's character the corrosive elements of self-pity which have caused Perry Miller and others to question her ability to be genuinely self-critical. Instead I find an intense and consistent attempt, from her early childhood onwards to be aware of her personal situation, to turn its crises and setbacks into positive directions, and to discover the truth about herself. This was often painful, and I can appreciate the temptation to turn aside from that pain and pretend that its expression is a self-indulgent character defect. In fact, when writing for herself or those she trusted (a smaller group than has traditionally been acknowledged — I would, for example, exclude Emerson from full membership from about 1842 onwards) the honesty and the refusal to compromise is stark and moving.

These personal records, and the substance of some of her dilemmas, — about vocation, about political action, about her lover and her family — give to Fuller's life an often startling modernity. Modern feminist scholars would no doubt like this to be matched by equally prescient and modern elements in her work, but are generally disappointed. (I have already explained why I think *Woman in the Nineteenth Century* was more important for what it was than for what it said.) Fuller's role as a landmark in the history of American and British feminism is a largely symbolic one. In modern theoretical and philosophical work about feminism she is conspicuous by her absence. She is in effect a founding mother without a legacy. On the broadest level this illustrates the tendency in modern feminist analysis to be insufficiently sensitive to the contextual possibilities of earlier bodies of feminist thought. The outcome, from which Fuller may have suffered, is a simultaneous underestimate of both the pressures of contemporary conventional thought and the extent to which tentative alternative formulations were genuinely revolutionary.

What is it about Fuller's work which makes it irrelevant to controversies in current feminist theory? One possible answer is Chevigny's 'way-station' theory: that Fuller worked through her feminism as a step towards the socialist convictions of her final years, and hence never returned to update and enrich it with the insights she gained in Paris and Rome.[2] As an explanation this can rebound. One of the key issues in contemporary feminism is its relationship with socialism. Fuller's own loyalties to the group interests both of women (which I have tried to show both predating and surviving after the success of *Woman in the Nineteenth Century*) and of the working class provides on one level a test case, almost exactly contemporaneous with the early work of Marx and Engels, of how women might be conceived of as a class. We just do not know how far she might have continued this project in further work, but there are clues that it would have featured significantly.

Another, more damaging, possibility is that her work is regarded from this perspective as at best unpalatable and at worst banal. Advocates of the abolition of slavery, of temperance, and of political reform in Rhode Island all learned the hard way about how difficult it was to enlist Fuller in coordinated political campaigns in Providence and Boston. Her approach as a journalist in New York was only a little more helpful as it oscillated between individual concern or appeals to philanthrophy and lofty reference to American national character. It was only really in Italy, out of sight of her more engaged American contemporaries, and (her letters and journalism apart) almost equally out of sight of posterity, that her skills as a committed member of a collective political movement emerged. By default therefore, the image of her as a writer and thinker that has endured is at best partial, at worst misleading. She survives principally as a romantic priestess at the altar of self-culture and moral self-improvement.[3] Given this as a perceived goal, and given the transcendentalist context in which it is usually set, it is hardly surprising that much of her work is seen as alien to the concerns of women in the twentieth century.

Fuller died at the age of forty. In the last year of her life, in spite of her pessimism and despondency at the failure of the Roman Revolution, she felt herself to be possessed of an understanding of major historical and political movements of a sophistication she had never before attained. We just do not know how she would have reflected upon and organised these in the major piece of writing she had begun in Italy. It is salutary to remember that had she lived she would have been fifty-one at the outbreak of the Civil War and fifty-three when Abraham Lincoln issued the Emancipation Proclamation. She would have been just sixty-one in the year of the Paris Commune, and the triumph of the Risorgimento, when Cavour (with unforeseen assistance from Garibaldi) realised Mazzini's dream of a reunified Italy. She had the potentiality of developing into a major figure in the relatively undistinguished pool of American socialist thinkers. Perhaps in this respect, far more than as a consequence of her unusual 'marriage', her friends were right to fear her return.

Similar speculation is possible in artistic spheres. We do not know, for example, how Fuller would have reacted to the mature work of Walt Whitman, a reading of which can demonstrate a range of leading ideas very similar to her own, including national destiny and sexual liberation. How too would she have read Herman Melville, with whom she is bracketted by Anne Rose as emblems of the road not taken towards a 'fully humanistic, historically minded romanticism'?[4]

It is precisely the open-ended quality of questions like these that has made Fuller a victim of successive and contradictory acts of appropriation and partial re-interpretation. These appropriations — by the editors of the *Memoirs*, by contemporary critics and artists like Hawthorne and James, by her biographers in the more sympathetic tradition of Higginson through Chipperfield, and by the feminist scholars of the last decade — have necessarily been as much a feature of this study (and have probably influenced it in ways I have been unable fully to control) as the life I have found revealed in the primary record. Each group has brought some illumination, even as it has been swept aside by the next cycle of revisionism, but overall I must conclude that the effect of using Fuller implicitly (and often primarily) for the purpose of self-definition by the writers concerned has been to distort her aims and her achievement.

I have structured this study in an attempt to expose these critical and historiographical problems. They are, of course, not unique to Fuller and may well be an inescapable feature of the art of biography. By separating analysis of Fuller's life, work and reputation I hope at least to have suggested a framework within which she can be approached which gives her an opportunity to speak for herself. I have also attempted a broader estimate of her legacy: as a contributor to definitions of American romanticism; as a feminist equally important for the strength and conviction of her observations about the condition of women as for the more dubious originality of her major feminist tract; and as a journalist (and finally a political commentator) of exceptional quality. All of these elements are necessary in the analysis and evaluation of her rich, complex, and tragically short life.

## Notes

1. *Memoirs*, III, pp. 229–30.
2. Chevigny 1976a, p. 222.
3. For an example of this type of analysis see Albert J. von Frank, 'Life as Art in America: The Case of Margaret Fuller' in Joel Myerson (ed.), *Studies in the American Renaissance*, Boston: G.K. Hall, 1981, pp. 1–26.
4. Rose, pp. 12–13.

# Chronology

1810     Born May 23, Cherry St., Cambridgeport.

1823     Attends Dr Park's School, Boston.

1824     Attends Miss Prescott's School, Groton.

1825     Family moves to Dana Mansion, Cambridge.
Attends Mr Perkin's Cambridge Port Private Grammar School.

1826     Timothy Fuller entertains John Quincy Adams.

1833     Family moves from Brattle Street to Groton.

1834     First publication in *The Daily Advertiser*.
July, expedition to Trenton Falls.

1835     1 Oct., death of Timothy Fuller.

1836     July, first visit to Emersons.
Dec., begins teaching at Alcott's Temple School.

1837     April – Dec. 1838, teaches at Greene Street Academy, Providence.

1839     Family moves to Jamaica Plain.
'Conversations' begin 6 Nov.
Publishes *Eckermann's Conversations with Goethe*.

1840     July edits first number of *The Dial*.
Aug. – Oct., crisis in relationship with Emerson.
Oct., marriage of Sam Ward and Anna Barker.

1842     Family moves to Ellery St., Cambridge.
July, hands over editorship of *Dial* to Emerson.
Publishes *Correspondence of Fraulein Günderode with Bettina von Arnim*.

1843     25 May – 19 Sept., western trip with James and Sarah Clarke.
July, family moves to Prospect Street.

1844     April, last of the 'Conversations'.
Finished writing *Woman in the Nineteenth Century*, with Caroline Sturgis at Fishkill, N.Y.
Dec., moves to Greeley's, Turtle Bay, N.Y.
Publishes *Summer on the Lakes*.

1845     June, James Nathan leaves for Europe.
Publishes *Woman in the Nineteenth Century*.

| 1846 | Moves to Brooklyn Heights. |
|---|---|
| | Publishes *Papers on Literature and Art.* |
| | Aug., sails for Europe with the Springs. |
| | Meets Mazzini, Carlyle and Wordsworth in England. |
| 1847 | Meets Mickiewicz and Sand in Paris. |
| | Travels to Genoa, Naples and Rome. |
| | April, meets Ossoli. |
| | Travels to northern Italy and Switzerland. |
| | Oct., returns to Rome, Via del Corso. |
| 1848 | Jan. and Mar., Italian uprisings. |
| | Feb., Ossoli's father dies. |
| | Summer in Aquila and Rieti. |
| | 5 Sept., Angelino born. |
| | Nov., returns to Rome, Piazza Barberini. |
| 1849 | Feb., Roman Republic declared. |
| | Mar., returns to Rieti. |
| | Apr. – June, siege of Rome, appointed to Hospital of the Fate bene Fratelli. |
| | July, returns to Rieti. |
| | Sept., visits Brownings in Florence. |
| 1850 | May 17, U S S *Elizabeth* sails. |
| | July 19, Fire Island Shipwreck. |
| 1852 | Publication of the *Memoirs of Margaret Fuller Ossoli.* |

# Bibliography

I have listed in Section A below the editions I have used of Fuller's works. Most of her published writings are now available in modern facsimile-style reprints. Each should be considered carefully in the context of its original production. For the reader who would like to sample Fuller's original work I would recommend, in order, *Summer on the Lakes*, *Woman in the Nineteenth Century*, and the second part of *At Home and Abroad*. The *Memoirs* obviously carry a major scholarly health warning, but they are worth dipping into not only for the revealing pieces of introduction and editorialising but also for some fragments which are not available elsewhere. *Love-Letters* includes three contemporary pen-portraits. Emerson's is lifted from the *Memoirs*, but the two by Greeley and Charles T. Congdon — trickier to obtain in their original form — reflect interestingly on Fuller's reputation as a journalist.

Fuller, like many of her contemporaries, lived an important part of her life through her letters. The first four of Hudspeth's intended five volumes of *The Letters of Margaret Fuller* are now published; the first three, up to 1845, were available to me. The edition is masterly, giving as full a set of contextual data for each item as is possible, and speculating sensibly and specifically where the information is elusive. For the other half of these important dialogues recourse can be made to the *Memoirs*, to the *Letters of Ralph Waldo Emerson*, edited by Ralph L. Rusk (New York: Columbia U. Press 1939), and to *The Letters of James Freeman Clarke to Margaret Fuller*, edited by J.W. Thomas. Care should be taken with the notes in the latter; at one stage 'Pia Nono' (sic) is identified as Mazzini!

Of the traditional-style anthologies two are frequently cited: those of Wade (1941) and Miller (1963). Each now shows its age but in its time represented an important act of recovery and rehabilitation. Perry Miller in particular has suffered cruelly, and I think unfairly, in the latest round of feminist revisionism. In the 1960s he was responsible, almost single-handed, for ensuring that the academic factory turning out new material on the transcendentalists took Fuller's contribution seriously.

118

Standing mid-way between anthology and biography is Bell Gale Chevigny's *The Woman and the Myth*. This work, which revolutionised Fuller scholarship in the mid '70s and did much to create the climate in which work like Paula Blanchard's and Margaret Allen's could be sensibly appraised, is essential reading. It will be apparent that I have used it, and Chevigny's other work, extensively, and disagree with its interpretations only in nuance.

I have commented in the text on the waves of revisionism represented by biographies of Fuller. A few more points are in order here. Thomas Wentworth Higginson's *Margaret Fuller Ossoli* is a vital, and frequently underacknowledged source for much of what we know of the American phase of Fuller's life. It is easy to dismiss Madeleine Stern's *The Life of Margaret Fuller* as falling into a genre of semi-fictional biography very much out of fashion today. But this conceals an immensely assiduous reconstruction of events in Fuller's life which, when the reader can summon up the discipline to ignore speculation about how the characters felt at the time, provides a powerful resource. Surveying the other biographies: Anthony's overt Freudianism probably has its most developed mid-century analogue in Wade's *Whetstone of Genius*; feminist advocacy achieves its height in Allen's *The Achievement of Margaret Fuller* and a more subtle voice in Blanchard's *Margaret Fuller: From Transcendentalism to Revolution*, recently released in paperback; of the other biographers, Julia Ward Howe, Margaret Bell and Faith Chipperfield each encapsulates a sentimental ideal-type of Fuller's life for its own time.

The secondary literature on or partly on Fuller has exploded in the last decade. Joel Myerson has been its most conscientious chronicler and the reader is directed to both his *Descriptive Bibliography* and the useful sample included in his *Critical Essays on Margaret Fuller*. In Section B I have listed only those books and articles of which I have made direct use, as indicated in the footnotes to each chapter.

## A Fuller's Writings

*Conversations with Goethe in the Last Years of His Life*, Boston: Hilliard, Gray, 1839

*Günderode*, Boston: Elizabeth Peabody, 1842

*Summer on the Lakes*, ed. Arthur B. Fuller, New York: Haskell House repr. of 2nd edn (1856), 1970

*Woman in the Nineteenth Century* (1845), intro. Bernard Rosenthal, New York and London: W. W. Norton repr. of 1855 edn, 1971

*Papers on Literature and Art*, 2 vols., London: Wiley & Putnam, 1846

*Memoirs of Margaret Fuller Ossoli*, 3 vols., ed. R. W. Emerson, W. H. Channing and J. F. Clarke, London: Richard Bentley, 1852

*At Home and Abroad, or Things and Thoughts in America and Europe*, ed. Arthur B. Fuller, Port Washington and London: Kennikat Press repr. of 1856 edn, 1971

*Life Without and Life Within; or, Reviews, Narratives, Essays, and Poems*, ed. Arthur B. Fuller, Upper Saddle River, NJ: Literature House/Gregg Press repr. of 1860 edn, 1970

*Art, Literature, and the Drama*, Boston: Brown, Taggard and Chase, 1860

*Love-Letters of Margaret Fuller, 1845–46*, intro. Julia Ward Howe, London: T. Fisher Unwin, 1903

'Margaret Fuller's 1842 Journal: At Concord with The Emersons' (incorporates full text of the journal), by Joel Myerson, *Harvard Library Bulletin*, 21 (1973), pp. 320–40

*The Letters of Margaret Fuller*, 5 vols., ed. Robert N. Hudspeth Ithaca and London: Cornell U. Press 1983– )

## B Anthologies, Biographies and Secondary Works

Allen, Margaret Vanderhaar, 'This Impassioned Yankee: Margaret Fuller's Writing Revisited', *Southwest Review*, 58 (1972), pp. 162–71

——, 'The Political and Social Criticism of Margaret Fuller', *South Atlantic Quarterly*, 72 (1973), pp. 560–73

——, *The Achievement of Margaret Fuller*, University Park and London: Penn. State U. Press, 1979

Anthony, Katherine, *Margaret Fuller: A Psychological Biography*, London: Jonathan Cape, 1922

Barbour, Frances M., 'Margaret Fuller and the British Reviewers', *New England Quarterly*, 9:4 (1936), pp. 618–25

Bell, Margaret, *Margaret Fuller: A Biography*, intro. Eleanor Roosevelt, Freeport, New York: Books for Libraries Press repr.

of 1930 edn, 1971

Blanchard, Paula, *Margaret Fuller: From Transcendentalism to Revolution*, New York: Delacorte/Seymour Lawrence, 1978

Braun, Fredrick A., *Margaret Fuller and Goethe*, New York: Henry Holt, 1910

Chevigny, Bell Gale, *The Woman and the Myth: Margaret Fuller's Life and Writings*, Old Westbury, New York: Feminist Press repr. 1976 [1975]

——, 'The Long Arm of Censorship: Myth-making in Margaret Fuller's Time and Our Own', *Signs*, 2:2 (1976), pp. 450–60

——, 'Growing out of New England: The Emergence of Margaret Fuller's Radicalism', *Women's Studies*, 5:1 (1977), pp. 65–100

——, 'Daughters Writing: Toward a Theory of Women's Biography', *Feminist Studies*, 9:1 (1983), pp. 79–102

——, 'To the Edges of Ideology: Margaret Fuller's Centrifugal Evolution', *American Quarterly*, 38:2 (1986), pp. 173–201

Chipperfield, Faith, *In Quest of Love: The Life and Death of Margaret Fuller*, New York: Coward McCann, 1957

*The Letters of James Freeman Clarke to Margaret Fuller*, ed. John Wesley Thomas, Hamburg: Cram, de Gruyte & Co., 1957

Cooke, George Willis, *An Historical and Biographical Introduction to Accompany the Dial*, 2 vols., New York: Russell & Russell repr. of 1902 edn, 1961

Cott, Nancy F., *The Bonds of Womanhood: 'Woman's Sphere' in New England, 1780–1835*, New Haven: Yale U. Press, 1977

Deiss, Joseph Jay, *The Roman Years of Margaret Fuller: A Biography*, New York: Thomas Crowell, 1969

*The Dial: A Magazine for Literature, Philosophy and Religion, 1840–44*, New York: Russell & Russell repr. 1961

Douglas, Ann, 'Margaret Fuller and the Search for History: A Biographical Study', *Women's Studies*, 4:1 (1976), pp. 37–86

——, *The Feminization of American Culture*, New York: Knopf, 1977

Durning, Russell E., *Margaret Fuller, Citizen of the World: An Intermediary between European and American Literature*, Heidelberg: Carl Winter Universitätsverlag, 1969

Ehrenreich, Barbara and Deidre, English, *For Her Own Good: 150 Years of the Experts' Advice to Women*, London: Pluto Press, 1979

*The Collected Works of Ralph Waldo Emerson, Vol. 1 — Nature, Addresses and Lectures*, ed. Robert E. Spiller and Alfred R. Ferguson, Cambridge, Mass.: Harvard U. Press, 1971

Feinstein, Howard, *Becoming William James*, Ithaca and London: Cornell U. Press, 1984

Flower, Elizabeth and Murray G. Murphey, *A History of Philosophy in America*, 2 vols., New York: G. P. Putnam's Sons, 1977

Frank, Albert J. von, 'Life as Art in America: The Case of Margaret Fuller', in *Studies in the American Renaissance*, ed. Joel Myerson, Boston: G. K. Hall, 1981, pp. 1–26

Hawthorne, Nathaniel, *The Blithedale Romance*, Harmondsworth: Penguin, 1986

Higginson, Thomas Wentworth, *Margaret Fuller Ossoli*, New York: Greenwood Press repr. of 1890 edn, 1970

Howe, Julia Ward, *Margaret Fuller*, Eminent Women Series, London: W. H. Allen & Co., 1883

Hoyt, E. A. and L. S. Brigham, 'Glimpses of Margaret Fuller: The Greene Street School and Florence', *New England Quarterly*, 29 (1956), pp. 87–98

Jones, Alexander E., 'Margaret Fuller's Attempt to Write Fiction', *Boston Public Library Quarterly*, 6 (1954), pp. 67–73

Matthiessen, F. O., *American Renaissance: Art and Expression in the Age of Emerson and Whitman*, New York and Oxford: Oxford U. Press, 1974 [1941]

Miller, Perry (ed.), *Margaret Fuller: American Romantic. A Selection from her Writings and Correspondence*, Ithaca: Cornell U. Press 1970 [1963]

——, *The Transcendentalists: An Anthology*, Cambridge, Mass.: Harvard U. Press, 1971 [1950]

Myerson, Joel, *Margaret Fuller: A Descriptive Bibliography*, Pittsburg: U. Pittsburg Press, 1978

——, (ed.), *Critical Essays on Margaret Fuller*, Boston: G. K. Hall, 1980

Norton, Anne, *Alternative Americas: A Reading of Antebellum Political Culture*, Chicago and London: U. Chicago Press, 1986

Rendall, Jane, *The Origins of Modern Feminism: Women in Britain, France and the United States, 1780–1860*, Basingstoke: Macmillan, 1985

Richardson, Robert D., *Myth and Literature in the American Renaissance*, Bloomington: Indiana U. Press, 1978

Rose, Anne C., *Transcendentalism as a Social Movement*, New Haven and London: Yale U. Press, 1981

Rosenthal, Bernard, '*The Dial*, Transcendentalism, and Margaret

Fuller', *English Language Notes*, 8 (1970), pp. 28–36

Smith-Rosenberg, Caroll, *Disorderly Conduct: Visions of Gender in Victorian America*, New York and Oxford: Oxford U. Press, 1985

Spender, Dale, *Women of Ideas and What Men Have Done to Them: From Aphra Behn to Adrienne Rich*, London: Routledge & Kegan Paul, 1983

——, *Feminist Theories: Three Centuries of Women's Intellectual Traditions*, Shoreditch: Women's Press, 1983

Stern, Madeleine B., *The Life of Margaret Fuller*, New York: E. P. Dutton, 1942

Strauch, Carl F., '"Hatred's Swift Repulsions": Emerson, Margaret Fuller and Others', *Studies in Romanticism*, 7:2 (1968), pp. 65–103

Taylor, William R., and Christopher Lasch, '"Two 'Kindred Spirits": Sorority and Family in New England, 1839–46', *New England Quarterly*, 36:1 (1963), pp. 23–41

Wade, Mason, *Margaret Fuller: Whetstone of Genius*, New York: Viking Press, 1940

——, (ed.), *The Writings of Margaret Fuller*, New York: Viking Press, 1941

Wellisz, Leopold, *The Friendship of Margaret Fuller D'Ossoli and Adam Mickiewicz*, New York: Polish Book Importing Co., 1947

Welter, Barbara, *Dimity Convictions: The American Woman in the Nineteenth Century*, Athens: Ohio U. Press, 1976

# Index

125